Beyond the Clouds

Louise M Smith

This Book Belongs to

Kingdom Builders

Publications

Library of Congress Control Number – 2013921848
ISBN – 978-0-578-12048-5

Photography – JWE Photography
Cover Designer – Gail Kyles
Beauty Consultant – Shavan Fulton
Makeup Artist – Avis Washington
Hair – Annie Ried's Creations
Onsite Stylist – JoAnn Ligons
Nails – Marie & Jeromé

Editors:
Wanda Brown
New Dawning Publications
The Late Angelois Smalls
Felicia Roberson
Kingdom Builders Publications

Go to our website: www.kingdombuilderspublications.com
Email us at: kbpublications@sc.rr.com

Dedication

This book is dedicated to the memory of my birthparents who thought it not robbery to let me exist; even if it meant perishing to the formative years of our relationship for a mere 30 years. The sacrifice did pay off because reunion with my birth mother blossomed into a 16-year love affair, with my birth father for 17 years, and my siblings an ongoing love affair. I gained my heritage with John Henry and Delores Simmons and ongoing sisterhood with Michelle, Jacqueline, Sandra, and Janine with other family members.

To the memory of Sam and Marie Merritts, Sr. my surrogate parents who also in their unwavering love reared me in the fear and admonition of the Lord and gave me opportunities in life that I might not have experienced otherwise. To my brother, Sam Jr., who was a very quiet influence in my life. Although there was a 23-year age difference between us, I admired his gift of basketball, visual art, and singing.

To my Aunt Lizzie and her late daughter Angelois (2013) who poured songs and living virtuously before a highly impressionable child. Thanks for the Sunday school choir experiences. To my Grandmother Mattie Sellers-Smalls-Sanders (Muncie Indian), who was my heroine in my upside down, right side up life. She was the one who was closest to truth like my Daddy. I adore you still.

To my wonderful children and their seed Maurice Bernard (Nikki), Carlisle JaVos (LaRessa), and Kendall; there can be no words to describe the admiration and adoration I have for you. You all are my absolute favorite! I praise God for every Monday, and Friday. You were born these days to your Pops & me. I am most blessed to see the replicas of you Maurice in Giana, Aswan, Caleb and Trinity and the same with Carlisle in Travis, Elsilrac and Asseral. I also acknowledge Carl Allen with his beautiful daughter, Dayjah.

I express my troth to the man of my life, Linton. He is in my spirit and soul and mind. He is the only other occupant that shares those secret places where God dwells. Thank you for choosing me to accomplish dreams with. Like my wedding band, there is no beginning or end to my affection and commitment to you.

To every spiritual mother, father, sister, brother, aunt, and uncle that has imparted to me the oracles of faith; and to the countless children that I have beaconed, thank you for sharing and receiving the wealth.

To my countless acquaintances, friends; and even my haters; I celebrate you and have learned from you all. After peeking into my memoirs, you can have a better appreciation for who I am. Without apology I am proud to be an American, Black and Christian. I can never be ashamed of my heritage anymore.

Finally, I could be nowhere in the walk without the guidance of the Pastors to whom I was called. I salute you Uncle and Pastor Willie Sellers. You were responsible for my placement in Christ's body through salvation at age 11, to Bishop Vincent and First Lady Chrystal Collins - powerhouses in the K.O.G. You continue to nurture and feed sheep; thanks for a great congregation and excellent pastoral care. To Pastor Eric B. Morris; the gentle giant who always let me see in him the calm persona of Jesus; To Pastor Gregory Sherman and Pastor Dana A. Holmes; you have help to change the course of my path in life with life-changing instruction, direction and example. Thank you; thank you all.

Louise Smith

Prologue

—~~—

This manuscript is a look into some of the dreams I believe GOD gave to me. I consider all of these dreams to be a gift to me from God. The providence of God is made known to me in some of these dreams as well as in real time. Various struggles and triumphs over the years have helped to prepare me for my specific task in the Kingdom. Before I was born, I was ordained to do specific exploits for the Lord. I will continue walking the fertile paths until I transition, taking as many as possible on the journey with me. I am being taken to new levels of worship and ministry.

We are all tripartite beings; spirit, soul, and body. We all are a spirit, we have a soul, and we all live in a body. The spirit represents the inner being of man. This is what people experience when one speaks a word or walks into a room. The essence of one's spirit is the mood and attitude. It represents the character and strength of oneself. Within the mind holds the emotions, will, imagination, and the intellect. The spirit and soul are used interchangeably, but are slightly different. The soul of a man houses the mind. Hebrews 4:12 reads "For the word of God is quick, and powerful, and sharper than any two-edged sword, piercing even to the dividing asunder of soul and spirit and of the joints and marrow, and is a discerner of the thoughts and intents of the heart." (The Word of God is not merely a collection of words from God, a vehicle for communicating ideas; it is living, life changing, and dynamic as it works in us. With the incisiveness of a surgeon's knife, God's Word reveals who we are and what we are not. It penetrates the core of our moral and spiritual life. It discerns what is within us, both good and evil. The demands of God's Word require decisions. We must not only listen to the Word, we must let it shape our lives.) (Life Application Study Bible) The body is the mortal shell that we see on a daily basis. It is comprised of bone, blood, mucus, cells, membrane, skin, tissue, ligament, vein, organs, and hair. If any one thing of this tripartite unit is out of kilter, the whole body is out of balance. Therefore, it would take great effort to pull all parts back to center and functioning properly again.

We all are familiar with the struggles of being out of our comfort zone. In the body, it is natural for the mind to coax the emotions into anxiousness. Nevertheless, in our souls, we could learn and practice the discipline of self-control. At moments when our practice is perfected, that is the moment we adhere to the point "be anxious for absolutely nothing." The Spirit Himself gives us the courage to go against our flesh and do the thing that is right, and we can do it without fear. Then we get a sense of overwhelming JOY as a reward of obedience to what is right! As humans, there is an absolute fight in our soul for control and power. The body wants domination as to the soul. The human spirit will act in accordance to what has been fed to it. There is a tug-of-war in the mind. The power struggle is in these questions (should I, could I, would I do evil or good?) The Spirit is alive unto God, and the flesh is always seeking its own victories over your human spirit and

God's Spirit. That's why the scripture was written, "Don't become so well-adjusted to your culture that you fit into it without even thinking. Instead, fix your attention on God. You'll be changed from the inside out. Readily recognize what he wants from you, and quickly respond to it. Unlike the culture around you, always dragging you down to its level of immaturity, God brings the best out of you, develops well-formed maturity in you" (Rom 12:2, The Messenger translation). As we submit to God and fix our attention on Jesus' lifestyle, the change begins to come in us. The relationship between God and man can be glorious. We all have our roles; the man side and the God side. The Lord's desire is to take us from faith to faith and from glory to glory. If allowed, God can be in control.

The first lesson of many is although God is sovereign, sits on the throne, and has all power, God will not force His will on you. However, if you allow God, He will perform his work through you. Be encouraged, and participate in your destiny! What God has for you (within the confines of your cooperation) you will have it! Do not cave in to erroneous thinking. This will surely lead to behavior that will send you on a downward spiral of consequences in bad decisions. You do not want that for you or your emotional circle (family and friends) and God, your Creator, certainly does not want that for you. This is why He admonishes you to choose blessings not curses; life not death; love not lust.

The second lesson here is not to esteem your gifts, talents, or ministry above the Lord and never ever should you substitute your works FOR God. Never let the works that you do for God substitute your relationship with God. Take into account first, that God is jealous of anything that replaces your personal time with Him. In other words, anything that resides in God's rightful place in your life will not allow God to help you in matters of the spirit, soul, and flesh. Everything you have please understand that you did not give it to yourself, The Lord, the Father of Lights, is the giver of every good and perfect gift. God is the core and the head of everything. God is Alpha and Omega, the beginning and the end. He's also everything in between. Use these truths as stepping stones for your success in the Kingdom of God. If you never forget these truths, you won't spend your days in fear, worry, doubt, unbelief, and lost opportunity. Remember, Seek ye first the Kingdom of God and his righteousness (everything that is right) and all these things will be added unto you (Matthew 6:33).

I pray with all my heart that every person, whether you are seeking a spiritual lifestyle or already have one, would realize and reach your fullest potential in this AWESOME KINGDOM OF EXCELLENCE. Our King is Excellent! He is the Lord; strong and mighty! He IS the King of Glory! He is mighty in Battle! Gaining Heaven is not just for having a diet of milk and honey, walking on gold streets, living in Heaven-sized mansions to fulfill God's purpose in the earth. To name a few, we were created to love, worship, progress, advance, and prosper. God's design for us is written in his Will, better known as the BIBLE (Basic Instructions before Leaving Earth). If we satisfy the Spirit of God by following these mandates set for us by Jesus the Testator, then He will be glorified, and we will have experienced the abundant life. May this be our prayer, Amen.

Introduction

Everybody has experienced dreams at one time or another. I'm not just speaking of dreaming as wishful thinking, imagination, or aspiration; these are daydreams of the things we see when we imagine something we want to do, be, or have. We can daydream with or without thoughts. I'm sure you're familiar of a moment when you wandered off in your mind, having a blank stare on your face. I have had this happen to me. As I regained consciousness, I could hear the person I was speaking with say, "Earth to Louise." I nervously laughed with embarrassment. When asked what I was thinking about, I had not a clue and was left wondering whether it escaped me or whether I was just absent for a while.

We play out scenarios in our mind through dreaming. What exactly is a dream? Scientists/Doctors declare that a dream is merely a sequence of mental images while one is sleeping. Many things can trigger a dream. Thoughts deep in the psyche, eating greasy and spicy foods, eating late at night, or seeing an image that buries itself in one's sub-conscience are all things people rationalize for having absurd or bizarre dreams. I have considered a trance to be another part of the sub-conscience experience. According to scripture, dreams were sometimes impressions on the minds of sleeping persons, made by divine agency. Many persons had dreams in the Scriptures. God came to Abimelech in a dream. God warned Joseph, Son of

Benjamin, Daniel, Aaron, and Miriam in a dream. The Lord also appeared to Solomon in a dream. There were many to have open dreams in the scriptures: Moses, John, Jacob, Peter, James, John the revelator, and Mary and her husband Joseph. We know that God truly uses dreams to deal with his people. In secular terms today, an open vision could be described as one being in a dazed or hypnotic state; hallucinations or delirium or being totally awake. Medical and psychology doctors treat the brain with drugs that either induce the results of dreams, hallucination, or delirium or rid the effects of them. Dreams are real. People in times past have had dreams that refer to the future. John, the revelator is noted in 21 chapters in the scriptures. I have had daydreams, night dreams, open (waking) visions, and I have been in trances. Not to sound spooky, but each was a different journey. When I was 36 years old, I was prescribed morphine for pain after I was seriously injured in a head-on car crash that broke both femur bones, almost severed the lower right leg, and left me with contusions about the face. While in the hospital, I had a vision (hallucinations) that men dressed in armor were jumping over my bed. Although drugs may have been responsible for that happening, I believe God was showing me how He was protecting me. I felt safe. I used to be frequently in transient states because of petit mal and grand mal seizures. There were conflicting diagnoses by doctors of epilepsy verses pseudo-seizures. When I was six years old, I was struck by a car while walking home from school. After a few months of healing from external scars, I started experiencing petit mal seizures. I was unable to be around running water or sirens because they seemed to pull me into a trance or petit mal seizures. One day while at recess with my second grade classmates, my body went limp. I fell to the ground and my body went completely out of control. I smelled fresh blood or something similar to that aura in my nostrils. For years after that I would have these episodes called grand mal seizures. Without notice, they would come upon me. At first I was put on a cocktail of Phenobarbital and Dilantin to control them, but at times nothing would control the activity. I went through many known concoctions over time for these fits of convulsions. When I was about ten years old, I would read the scriptures about the man who was called lunatic and thought that I was genetically connected to him. My peers were afraid of me; they would scorn and jeer me. It seemed so hopeless for a young girl full of life and music to be stricken with such an infirmity. Those trances were not inspired by the Spirit of the Living God, but rather by the spirit of infirmity. At the time I didn't know about the spirit of sickness or infirmity, but I knew it was weird for a believer to be stricken with such a violent sickness. I remember when singing a song like "Yes Jesus Loves Me", it wasn't quite making sense to me. God being a Savior and healer was a bit confusing to me. I never rejected God, church, religion, or faith because these were the things that got me through the really rough spots; however, I knew something was missing. I just didn't have all the facts for my healing. I gathered from wrong teaching that it was acceptable to be sick because that showed that God was getting glory from my life of sickness. I later learned that no sickness had anything to do with God getting glory out of my or anyone else's life; especially after He healed the lunatic in the scriptures. Today, like the lunatic, I am completely and forever healed of those tormenting seizures.

Perhaps by reading this book of inspirational dreams and visions, you will see that God's desire for all mankind is for us to be restored back to our first state before sin, in a true relationship with God, obeying and loving Him. God gives us windows and doors of opportunity to know Him and to know His intentions for our existence.

God's Word is very clear on this matter. Do not ignore the Savior's calling. Remember, the only thing that will ever stop you from getting to God and sowing Him in the earth among your family, peers, and new friends is YOU!

Come and journey with me amid the clouds, but don't just keep your head in the sky, seek and find the revealed plan for your life. God knows, "for I know the thoughts that I think toward you, saith the LORD, thoughts of peace, and not of evil, to give you an expected end" (Jeremiah 29:11). Focus on the duties assigned you from the Kingdom of Heaven for the people of Earth. There is a world, a celestial shore that the redeemed will retire to when the work is completed. The Master Himself will give the command. Archangel thunder! God's trumpet blast! He'll come down from Heaven and the dead in Christ will rise--they'll go first. Then the rest of us who are still alive at the time will be caught up with them into the clouds to meet the Master (1Th 4:16-17, The Messenger Translation). In the meantime, get to work preparing ungodly people to become a godly people of faith, mission hope and purpose. It is the mandate of every believer to populate the Kingdom of God and prepare for Heaven.

Chapter One
The Raven

⸙

    This could be taken as a strange and a bizarre dream, but almost immediately I understood the interpretation of this dream. It blessed me in such a way and I never forgot it. One day in my mother's house (I was sixteen at the time) I remembered having a dream that moved me so much that I wrote it down. I thought about what I saw, and I knew that God was inspiring a message in me. This is the only dream of this sort I had as a teen. The other dreams came after I became an adult. I dreamed that I was in my bedroom brushing my hair when suddenly I felt a breeze from the window. Though it was abnormal, I was enjoying this refreshing draft. From this wind blew in a dark bird resembling a raven that perched on my shoulder. Although its appearance looked frightening, I felt no threat by it. The bird appeared highly intelligent, as if he could talk. I stroked it and tried to get it to perch on my finger. When my eye met this fowl, I began to lose my confidence. Its eyes looked as though they knew my whole life story and would reveal it without hesitation. The thought alone was frightening; as frightening as his sharp beak close enough that it could at any moment pierce my eye. But a surge of faith rose up in me taking away the fear. I became emotionally prepared for the moment the bird flew onto my hand. Without hesitation or warning, its head turned into the head of an infant child. I suddenly felt that I was giving birth. I felt joy. The key elements or symbols of this dream were:

☐ **Brushing my hair** – Grooming for the task before me; to be set apart as a servant)

☐ **Raven** – Intelligent in character; God used the raven to feed the Prophet Elijah flesh and water. The Word of God is the Living Bread and Living Water, and since I hunger and thirst for God; I must seek, find and devour the Word. I will be filled.

☐ **the predisposition of giving birth** – What is more precious than an infant; God wants us all in that position of "His Children." A baby is a pure soul alive unto God without the consciousness of sin. My responsibility is to feed the children with what I have devoured: a living diet of bread and water! The Word is alive; it is Spirit and it is Life! The truth of God was incubated in me because of my hunger for the Word. I am impregnated with His spirit and am giving birth to the call He has spoken in me.

Chapter Two
Learning the System

At an early age, I had a very real sense of God. I always knew that I loved Him even though I never saw Him. I learned about God and could imagine Him while in Sunday school. I could imagine God while the preacher was preaching, or when someone would give a testimony of the workings of God saving, healing, or doing something fantastic. Sam and Marie adopted me in the 50's. They were the first to introduce me to Jesus. They were devout Christians in every sense of the word. I would hear beautiful songs in the Sunday school choir, and different inspirational songs of the gospel choir. I loved them all. Even though I was never allowed to play, as my mother called them, REELS, or secular songs, I didn't really miss them because I loved God songs. I recall at around age four, I would mimic piano players on the oil heater. I would position my fingers on it as if I were playing a real piano. Its tin sound was so beautiful; it sounded like music. In fact all flat surfaces were my platform for piano music. I was practicing to play the piano. It is the instrument I have played since the age of five. I remember how I would build a stage coach out of my parents' lawn chair. I would climb up in it to drive the imaginary horses and sing Clara Ward's "Packing Up Getting Ready to Go." My imitation of the words was hilarious; nevertheless, I was struck by the words of that song. Other songs like "I Come to the Garden Alone," "Where He Leads Me," and "Just As I Am" would bring me to tears at the tender age of four. I would listen to the songs sung by choirs at the C.O.G.I.C. tent revivals in our neighborhood. I remember vividly "The Lord is Blessing Me Right Now," which was my first solo in church. I would have child experiences that would comfort and assure me that Jesus was real.

I have always loved the privilege of going outside and getting in the hammock. For as many times as I fell out trying to get in, those were times of extreme solace and happiness for me. With a strong history of epilepsy, it was hard for my mother to allow me to be alone, but during those times I could go outside, I would play in the hammock, or with the lawn furniture. I would gaze up in the clouds and try to see Jesus, but it never really happened that way. I knew He existed because I would see people respond to Him in church by coming to the altar or shouting and dancing or speaking in the heavenly language. Oh, I knew He existed. My parents' son, Junior, as he is affectionately called, is 23 years my senior. We were both raised as only children. Our parents were well to do middle-class coloreds. My dad worked for the railroad and the shipyard, and my mother was a nurse's assistant for the SC Crippled Children's Home; prior to that my mother was a domestic worker. My brother and I lacked for absolutely nothing – well, except affection from our mother. Life was great, life was horrible, and life was weird. I had the connection to God, but I could not connect to the world. I was not liked by my peers, and most strangely, my imagination sensed the same with my brother and mother. I was clumsy, naive, and sickly, and that is putting it mildly. Some even called me ugly. People liked when I would sing and play the piano. I was referred to as the entertainer but as a person, it seemed people could not connect with me. I could hardly fit their mold. Boys picked at me and girls beat me up. We all endure something hard in life but in order to survive, we make the adjustments and we move on! Going through things in life helps to form character and integrity. In the next few dreams, I hope to show how God's presence brought me calm through some of my most strenuous experiences. God is my providence; I should never be afraid. My part of the bargain was to keep my mind on Him. I already knew I would win.

Chapter Three
Spiritual Dormancy

———∿∿∿———

I remember so vividly being 21 and had just recently given birth to my second child, Carlisle. I was the musician for a little country church Mount Pisgah in Mars Bluff, SC. The church was formerly named Sand Beige Baptist Church. This is the church of my Daddy's ancestry Elliot and Janie Durant Merritts. I was not fortunate to have met my father's parents for they had died before I was born. My grandparents had eight children. Sam was the firstborn. My father Sam Merritts married my mother Marie Smalls on August 12, 1934 and moved uptown to Florence in 1935 after the birth of their only surviving birth child Sam Junior. They were in their early 20s. Sam Sr, his wife, and son moved their membership to Saint Peter Holiness Church of the Believers Movement in West Florence, SC. I was grandfathered in as a member through adoption. In my early 20's, I relinquished my membership there and fellowshipped at a neighborhood church close to our home.

Mount Pisgah Baptist Church was the place where one could find me every second and fourth Thursday evening and Sunday morning of the month. One particular month, Mount Pisgah was celebrating its church anniversary. All ministries were making ready for their participation in the annual shindig, to include the choir. The choir wanted to present a good musical program for the Sunday morning worship. The choir and I worked about five hours each week. This was about two and half hours each Thursday and Saturday. We were almost at the day of celebration. The choir had ordered new burgundy robes, flamboyant in style. These robes had big puff sleeves with pleats,   a layered tunic with a treble sign circled in metallic gold. The choir director's robe was the opposite of the group's design. His robe color was metallic gold with a burgundy sash.

It was Anniversary Sunday morning, 10:40, the Sunday school had ended and the various organizations assembled in groups for prayer and service. The choir was positioned in the back of the church for the procession. It is now 11:00 a.m., and the music begins. The choir director comes in, the congregation stands, and the Pastor gives the call to worship. The Mount Pisgah Young Adult Choir comes in with a BANG! They were swaying and displaying their new robes and new sound. Folk in the congregation were very responsive to their look and song. Their claps and shouts seemed to be perfect praise. I was on the piano playing the song and enjoying the moment, when suddenly…I am in the spirit. I am having a vision; my eyes are wide open and yes while playing the piano in church, I see a totally different scene. I was looking over the congregation where people were clapping and shouting but the Lord revealed to me something different. Some of them were *sleeping.* I singled out individuals such as a woman standing over a range stirring what looked like dried up oatmeal. She was a*sleep.* There was another woman with a hairnet that held in her falling rollers; her bathrobe slightly shrouding her body. She was standing over a bed as if to make it, but she was…*asleep.* I saw a man who had on a black and burgundy small polka-dot smoking jacket. He was set in a recliner. He was as you guessed it, *asleep.* Please note that while I am seeing this with my own eyes, church is shonuff going on, and the commotion of church is happening. I see yet another person, a child, lying across the bed, dressed up for church but she was…asleep. By now the choir is almost in place on the choir stand. I am the only one seeing what I'm looking at. I'm watching the congregation and nothing is really changing. My eyes are now on the choir members. They were as lively as could be, some even gyrating in the choir pew. There were some members standing…completely *dormant*. I looked in the pulpit. The Pastor had on a green colored sun visor with a pearl colored cigarette holder. The cigarette was lit. There were gobs and gobs of coins and currency at his feet, but he was…in a *coma*. I was flabbergasted. The thing that perplexed me the most was my apparent out of body experience. I was looking myself, and what do you think I saw? I saw me, slumped over the piano; hands on the keys, and I was indeed, *asleep*.

I could barely finish playing the processional selection. The opening hymn was "We've Come This Far by Faith." I managed to stay on the keyboard to finish the hymn, prayer, and prayer chant. As soon as the music was finished, I quickly exited the sanctuary. My eyes were blinded with tears. I was truly terrified! I didn't know what God was trying to say, but I knew He was trying to say something!

A month prior, I decided to have two rehearsals weekly. Carl, my "wasband" said to me, "Why do you let people take advantage of you? People know that you are good and you love what you do. But you have a family-- two small children. You need to get paid for your services. Now, Shirley Caesar never sings a note without getting her money. You need to tell these people you need your money." Carl was not a religious man, so he was perhaps speaking out of greed instead of out of need. He was not an authority on matters of the church. Carl had a job and I was getting a stipend twice a month from the church. I was pleased with it because I was doing what I greatly loved and what I was sure God placed in me to do. However it is amazing what seeds get planted in your thinking. You may think things you hear do not affect you, but it goes in your ear gate and into your belly; take root and soon you could take action. The words of a gossip are swallowed greedily, and they go down into a person's innermost being (Proverb 18:8).

It seemed like an innocent request so one Thursday night after rehearsal, one of the choir members was about to take me home when I began to make a request for some money. I felt that I needed to make an excuse to validate my request. I said to the president of the choir, "My baby needs some milk and it would be good for me to have a little extra money for some pampers." I was really nervous that I would be rejected, but surprisingly they jumped in to grant my request. I thought to myself, "Wow that was easy! Was that all to it? I could've had this much sooner than now!" They all took up an offering, and gave me about 25 bucks. Carolyn, my first cousin and officer of the choir said that a collection would be the standard for the choir to give me at every rehearsal because they appreciated my hard work and talents. Wow. I began quoting the Bible to justify my actions: "Ask and it shall be given" but something was tugging on the inside of me. My request seemed harmless. Calvin was usually my ride back and forth to rehearsals since Carl worked at nights and drove our vehicle. He was also an officer of the choir in the decision making progress with Carolyn. Afterwards, Calvin and his wife drove me to the Piggly Wiggly and bought the disposable diapers and milk before taking me home. I didn't even have to spend the $25 they took up for me. People quote the Bible saying "a man is worthy of his hire." Remember I said I was already getting a stipend from the church. Did I really need to get money from the choir as well? Yes, it was easy to obtain, but that was not for me to request. The Lord was supplying my needs through my husband and the two churches where I was the musician. My financial needs, for the most part, were being met.

Let me take you back to the bathroom where I wound up. My eyes were drowned in tears. I cried out to God to help me and to show me the revelation of this sight. He sounded like mad and raging waters. "I am God. You can NEVER substitute anything for me; not your talent, not your money. I am YOUR source; everything else is a resource. I supply all your need and all you need is ME! Have you ever gone hungry? Have you ever gone without shelter? Have you gone without money? Am I God? Will you exchange money for health? Will you trade money for joy or peace of mind? Will you substitute worldly gains for my anointing? STAND SURE BEFORE ME. Be pure before me. Bring your praise and your presents to me. I will give the increase." The Lord talked extensively to me that fourth Sunday morning in June 1979. I sobbed sorely and repented before the Lord. He forgave me that moment, but because I wanted to please the Lord and to make sure I was not in disobedience. I committed not to sing or play the piano again until I was absolutely sure WHY I was doing it. I didn't want to do it because I had ability, because I could get monetary gain, or because I was asked. I wanted to glorify God and be a blessing to the people without being a common church whore. (doing it just for the money, or because "so and so" asked to do it, or because I had a talent). God called on me that day and challenged me to be more because He had given me more; but the servant who didn't know what his master wanted and did things for which he deserved punishment will receive a light beating. A lot will be expected from everyone who has been given a lot. More will be demanded from everyone who has been entrusted with a lot (Luke 12:48, God's Word translation). He called me and set me apart to be a worshipper, a songster, a Levite, and minstrel. I had to be careful about everything I said and did. Even my thought life was challenged. I got it wrong SO many times in each area of my life, but God in His sovereign, gave me mercy and compassion, forgave me and granted me chance upon chance to learn the lesson and get it right. I began to understand how to walk out my life and surrender to God wholly. I will be forever in that process until His return.

For a little over a year, I did not sing in any church, I did not play in any church even though I faithfully attended church and was a devoted student of the Lord's doctrine. I was being pruned and groomed. One Sunday in August 1980, while pregnant with my third son, Kendall, a woman approached me about being a special guest at her church on an afternoon program. The name of her church was Carver Street Baptist Church. I later became the full-time musician for that parish for nine and a half years. She told me that she heard me sing and play at New Ebenezer Baptist Church some time ago and had never heard anyone or felt anyone like that before or since. I was humbled by her compliment. I thought about my vow not sing or play. I wasn't sure if it was time yet, so I told her I would think about it and I would get back to her. I committed it to prayer. Then I had to trust God to help me know when I could go forth. She asked me again would I consider being on program at their church event. I felt released in my spirit to participate in the service. I didn't prepare a song to sing I did nothing but show up to the service. Early in the program, Juanita, the woman who invited me to the program, called me for a song. My stomach began to get butterflies. I stood and walked over to the piano. I didn't know at the time whether I would sing acapella or whether I would play the keys, but I remember lifting my hands to praise my God. I opened my mouth. The song "The Blood Will Never Lose Its Power," came pouring out of me; out of my soul. I couldn't believe my ears. God had changed my sound. He changed my tone. He changed my song. Because I changed my mind on certain things about worship and service and lifestyle, He changed my heart. I shall never forget that day. I teach everywhere I go and in my private music tutorials that God isn't looking for a Lucifer spirit, but rather a servant's heart. No matter how talented you think you are, there is always someone more talented than you. Therefore, what the Lord seeks is your true commitment and worship to Him. He gives all that we need, but it is never for ourselves alone. It is always for others around us, and those we pursue. Don't get stuck in your ability, it's nothing without the blessing and power of God. Don't be tricked into spiritual whoredom. Guard your heart and your gift. "Do not give what is holy to dogs---they will only turn and attack you. Do not throw your pearls in front of pigs---they will only trample them underfoot" (Matthew 7:6). Satan was created to be a musician and he was a worshipper. In fact, pipes were made in him according to Ezekiel 28:13. Thou hast been in Eden the garden of God; every precious stone was thy covering, the sardius, topaz, and the diamond, the beryl, the onyx, and the jasper, the sapphire, the emerald, and the carbuncle, and gold: the workmanship of thy tabrels and of thy pipes was prepared in thee in the day that thou was created. Trust me when I tell you Satan is jealous of any worshipper because the true worshipper has his job. So, to destroy the works of music in the body of Christ, the devil will use you up by going this place and that place, by not blessing the people, by not effecting a change in anyone, and by not bringing glory to God. He will also cause the lust of the eyes, the lust of the flesh, and the pride of life to sift you with such things as fortune, fame, and ego. Don't get me wrong, you can be a Christian, serve the Lord to the fullest of joy, and have wealth, confidence, and be known all around the globe. However, you must be savvy of the devil's vices. He is a counterfeiter. He'll make things look like it is from God and it's a blessing to God, to people and to you, but in actuality, it's destroying your spirit, soul, and body. Always challenge your attitude. Love is not puffed up, and is not envious. Love is not vanity. Are you a servant? Are you doing it just to get money, or does money come to you because you carry the Gospel? Do you push yourself; exalt yourself or your own personal agenda and call it "ministry"? Careful now! Jesus never exalted Himself. He only exalted His Father and His fame still went out before Him EVERYTIME. We are still talking about Him today. We must humble ourselves and in due time, God will exalt us. (I Peter 5:6) Let me define the word ministry from a different perspective. Ministry is an office in which you administer help. As we use ministry relative to church, we assist the Pastor as he administrates the work of the church. We all assist the Lord in carrying the gospel to the lost and down trodden (workers together with Christ – I Corinthians 3:9 and II Corinthians 6:1). Recently I have been noticing the phrase "my ministry." Everybody seems to be saying this these days. I have even said it myself. We all know what we mean when we say, "my ministry" but sometimes piety shows in the hearts of some thus ministry becomes something other than the pure intent of the word. By this I mean the taking on of the Lucifer spirit found in Ezekiel 27 and 28. Ministry is just a colloquial for the assignment God gives an individual. Let "your" ministry be horizontal and vertical and never be centered; self-centered, that is. Hang personal ambitions, vanity, greed and arrogance on the "TREE!" Ministry is designed to help to administer aid to others. If you're doing ministry just for the dollars, it won't pay. Then the Bible says, "You have your reward!" Don't be deceived. Pastors, musicians and anyone who works full-time for the church should be compensated for their time and gifts. The distinguishing factor is ministry comes first and hard work supplies the income. The other factor is money comes first so it's just a survival tool to look like "ministry." Know the difference. Don't let your mind and flesh deceive you. Know the Word and know your calling. Ministry is not glamorous; it's not a get rich quick plan. The flesh is a mess according to the words of Paul in Romans 7:18. We must be a servant with a servitude heart. It must be a personal choice to help, bless, and esteem others (Philippians 2:3, International Standard Version) - Do not act out of selfish ambition or conceit, but with humility. Think of others as being better than yourselves; be relevant and evident in order to have a successful walk, holding back nothing for God, for fellow believers and for potentials.

Chapter Four
Calamity Accosted – Calm Released

My first long night dream as an adult was a trip my sons and I took to Virginia to visit family. It was 1985. We stayed on a boat house on the Chesapeake River with my cousin. In the dream, it was customary that all children attend school on weekends; whether they are residents or not. We had arrived on a Friday. The next morning, I cleaned the boat house in exchange for coming unannounced and not having many resources. My cousin Mae took all children to school early by way of her small motor boat. I got so engrossed in dusting and sweeping until I didn't realize that time had flown past 3:00 p.m. I was thinking they all must have stopped into town for shopping. School was recessed at 1:00 pm. Mae finally returned with the boys a little past four. My first born was the first face I saw since the morning's departure. He came through the door saying, "Hi Mommy, whatcha doing?" In my mind I was astonished that time had really flown. I responded, "I'm wonderful, darling and how are you? Where is Carlisle?" At that very moment, Mae walked through the door with tears in her eyes and looking in complete shambles. Maurice spoke without a care, sympathy or commiseration, "Oh you didn't know? Carlisle is dead! He got drowned!" Immediately I woke up in panic and total disarray. Sensing my panic, I was shaken and told by my friend CJ to wake up. Instantaneously, I began to speak of the horrific dream. She assured me that it was only a dream. Almost immediately after I had the dream, I called my birth mother in Charleston (better known by its residents as Chuck Town) telling her my early morning horror. After sharing, she shared her dream with me. Her dream was about her deceased mother who was visiting with her and my son, Carlisle. She came expressly to place a man's hat on her grandson's head. Momma thought it strange because she felt that was an omen of gloom and doom. She quickly took the hat off Carlisle's head and inquired why this thing was done to the boy. There was no answer before she vanished in the air. My dream was Wednesday and hers was Tuesday the week prior. The following Friday, I had another dream. This dream was in Charleston, the place where my children now have the opportunity that I would never have as a child; to reside with my family. In the dream, I bought a van. I was so happy to own a car that the first place I would go was Charleston. This in my mind would prove that I was well and independent. When I drove up to my parents' home, I tooted the horn so they might guess who I was, and come greet me. When my mother came and saw that it was me, she lit into me saying, "Oh I know you didn't! You drove way up here, BY YOURSELF???" Feeling her excitement as highly as mine, (thinking positively) I said, "Yeah, can you believe it?!" All at once, she rushed in the house, in great frustration she broke off not just a limb of a tree, but a whole tree to chastise me. I saw the fire in her eyes, which I had mistaken for great joy and happiness.   I said, "Momma, what's wrong?" She was frank in her reply, "Child you know you have problems. You don't take a venture like this without someone's knowledge of your whereabouts or someone to travel with you. I'll just bet a slew of folks are worried about you in Florence. I hope they're not thinking I coerced you into this ridiculous excursion." Totally washed in tears from my mother's words, and the guilt of not thinking my adventure through, I woke up to a numb feeling. I had felt so badly and punished for the act, it carried over when I woke up. Awake now, I called Charleston just to say hello to whoever would answer the phone. I needed to be stroked and feel love; not the failure I had just experienced in the dream. My dear friend at the time was in the shower preparing for work. She was totally oblivious to the call I was about to make. It would change everything about the day. My birth dad answered the phone (which was quite unusual that time of morning). My dad was a cabbie. He ran from 2:00 am until 10:00 am. I called the house around 7:00 a.m. When I greeted him, I said how surprised I was that he would be home that time of morning. He sounded peculiar. He sounded weary. But in his smooth deep tone, "Ah, everything is doing... well I thought you would have been here by now. Man, your momma's at the hospital there with Carlisle." I could not take another breath. Reflectively, I thought of the dream I had...I'm thinking doom! I had already been forewarned. I had already felt it. My Daddy said, "Ah, you ain't know? Carlisle got hit by a truck. I thought you knew. Fear tried to overtake me, but I had an extraordinary sense of calm. I didn't yell nor have any delirium over the phone. When Carolyn got out of the shower, she overheard me speaking to my Dad. She was taken aback by what she overheard me say over the phone. She didn't know how I would respond to her not revealing this information. She had received it on Wednesday, two days prior. I was a part-time student at a technical school and it was to be my first exam that Friday morning. Her thought was that she would hold confidence until after my exam, and then she would tell me while taking me to see Carlisle. When I saw my seven-year-old child who had been struck by a utility truck in my parents' neighborhood, I saw the providence of the Lord yet again. The flesh from Carlisle's leg was literally peeled from the bone. Amazingly and miraculously, the bone was never broken. His leg healed from the wounds and without serious repercussions. I believe God used that dream to warn me of danger and to allow me to feel it. He also gave me His peace. I had great calm. Through the prayers of the saints on both my mother's and son's behalf, the Lord gave our family a good report. The dream initially showed me a particular end, but my faith fueled forward and we prevailed. Things will happen if prayer is involved, and things will not get done if someone doesn't reach Heaven. I never doubted the Lord. I kept my mind and He kept my heart. And the peace of God that passes all understanding, shall keep your hearts and minds through Christ Jesus (Philippians 4:7).

Chapter Five
Mistaken Identity

———∿∿———

I was a young adult when I had a dream. This one was about three places – Columbia, South Carolina, an unknown city in Georgia and Detroit, Michigan. A couple of the places I dreamt about, I was now living out. I married a man from Georgia after moving to Columbia. I have yet to experience destiny's pull in Detroit. I know my destiny will lead me there some day.

The dream continues to the scene of my boys and me moving. The place felt like Georgia. We had very little possessions. All that we owned fit on the back of a pick-up truck. Our new place of residence was a duplex apartment with stairs that had an opening at the back of the staircase. As we were headed towards the duplex to our new abode, I was brushed by a huge grungy old man who for some strange reason thought he knew me. He spoke in a harsh accusatory tone, "It's YOU!" I responded, "Hello Sir, how are you. Have we met? I'm sorry I don't remember. I'm just moving here from another state." He came at me more harshly than before, "I don't believe it. You came back to this same spot?" I exclaimed, "Sir, you must be mistaken" "Oh, no! I ain't mistaken. There's just one thing I want to say to you; I'm gonna KILL you. You are responsible for the death of my wife, and I'm gonna KILL you! I was frightfully shocked he thought I was someone else. I thought I could convince him he was grossly mistaken. I replied, "Oh, Mister, I don't know you or your wife. Again, I am just moving here from another state. Surely you have me pegged for someone who looks a lot like me. I'm not who you think I am. The hostile and bitter man said, "Yeah, uh-ha, mmm-hmm. Yeah. Right, sure. But I'm STILL gonna kill ya." My children were not in sight of the man nor a threat to him. They had gone up before me to carry luggage and boxes. The man hastened away in a rage. His face showed destructive confidence; displaying hardness and coldness, and disconnect from humanity. As scared as I felt, I continued up the stairs to our new home. I unpacked some things trying to figure the whole matter of what just happened trying not to look unnerved. I began cooking our first meal when there was a rap on the door. It was a petite woman. I trusted that she was not a decoy to harm us. I cautiously opened the door as she told me she was from the lower floor. She seemed wise and settled. Although she spoke in a soft voice, she didn't come to welcome us but to warn us. She warned, "He's coming by midnight. Leave and go quickly." How could she have known my dilemma? I considered her a prophet, and took her heed. I left at eleven, one hour earlier. As I prepared us for escape trying to be inconspicuous, I bump into the very man I was trying to evade. It appeared he had been scheming my demise all of his life and was ready to carry it out two hours before midnight. He was armed for me, a defenseless woman, with killing gear that was fit for war – every kind of war paraphernalia. As we collided, we realized the time of death was imminent for someone. I commenced to run as fast and hard as I could. He then shot; missing but very close to target. Out of nowhere I gained momentum. In the momentum, I turned and started towards him. Quickly I was up on him. Faster than imaginable, I wrestled him to the ground and without any weapon I conquered the hostile man, threw his sword, grabbed his gun and shot him in the head.

I woke from this dream feeling like a criminal; even forsaken. How could I have dreamt such horror? Anyone's life being snuffed out cannot be a good thing, even if it's in a dream. All day I pondered and prayed for a revelation. As I relied on the Holy Ghost to give me insight, the words came to me. "SATAN IS SENT IN THE EARTH TO KILL, STEAL AND DESTROY, BUT I HAVE GIVEN YOU AUTHORITY TO BRUISE, EVEN MORE TO BRING DEATH TO HIS VICES. YOU HAVE THE AUTHORITY TO PLAN AND ACCOMPLISH YOUR LIFE." Then the scriptures Hebrew 2:14 and I John 3:8 came alive in my spirit. Forasmuch then as the children are partakers of flesh and blood, he also himself likewise took part of the same; that through death he might destroy him that had the power of death, that is, the devil (Hebrews 2:14). He that committeth sin is of the devil; for the devil sinneth from the beginning. For this purpose the Son of God was manifested, that he might destroy the works of the devil (1 John 3:8).

Dreams inspire and alert. We live in a world filled with trials and tribulation but Jesus has overcome the world. Tribulations cause turbulence but we can ride above the turbulence like the plane in a storm or an eagle facing brutal winds. I choose to soar high above the clouds. I know Christ is there to guide me as long as I abide. I thank my God for what He has given me. Satan uses his tactics THE BAG OF

SUGGESTIONS. This is his ONLY power. "Your dreams will die, you're not strong, you're sick." If you don't know the truth about God, His Son or yourself, you will give away your power. He is out for your destruction, but be reminded that you always win. The Lord fights for you that through death He might destroy him that had the power of death, that is, the devil.

Chapter Six
Eye in the Storm

September 25, 1993, I was scheduled to go to a youth explosion in a town called Hemingway. It was a small hometown pavilion. We were asked to participate in the function sponsored by the Bahá'í faith. Although I am a devout Christian, I didn't take notice of any strange practices or notice that some people didn't know or even honor God my Christ, especially in our Black heritage. I subscribed to Christianity, and thought that most Americans did too. The Children's Choir was on program to sing. I, along with Kendall and my friend Carolyn drove up to Hemingway. All the way to the center, we listened to Lisa Page's song, "Then My Lord Will Carry Me Home" on the car cassette player. The function went on so long, that Carolyn had to go home to take care of her ailing mother. I couldn't leave at the time, for my keyboard was on stage being used by other groups. Finally shortly after 11:30 p.m. we were breaking the stage down, cutting off lights to head home. I had to ride home with my neighbor Nelson; the same person who was responsible for us being on program. He was driving a Nissan Hatchback. I put the keyboard in the back with Kendall and I got in on the front passenger side. I remember feeling extremely exhausted this Friday night. It was a little after 12:00 midnight. I was wearing my favorite skirt and blouse, and gold slippers. I leaned down to take off my shoes, so that I could nap a little before getting home. Getting comfortable for about a thirty-five minute ride, when suddenly I heard the sound of crashing glass, then I felt the car. We were hit, and the car without flipping over spun several times; perhaps about five times (five IS the number of Grace). We were in the middle of nowhere; a dark country road at the intersection of an aisle. There was no one who had a phone on their person. It was really bad. There was only one other car in sight; the drunk that hit us head on. His name was Norman C. He was grieving for his deceased wife so he gets into a car without registration, tags, license, insurance or sobriety. When the car finished spinning, he came over totally inebriated bowing and bending saying, "Y'all okay? Y'all okay?"

At this time, I noticed that I could not feel my legs, I tried to move them, but they would not respond. The impact caused both my legs to be injured. Both femurs were broken and I had a huge gash that almost severed my right leg. Then I noticed Kendall had a different sound. He was snoring, but a totally different sound. It was a very deep snore. Nelson, who was the driver, was scarred on his knee, a small gash on his head and a seat belt burn. Kendall was knocked out of his seat into the hatchback, with open head contusions. He was knocked unconscious. He was later declared in a coma. I was semi-unconscious. There was glass all in my face. There was blood from my right leg and face. Kendall had bleeding from his head. I did not expect to live till morning. Who could help us at this highway isle? There was no hint of traffic, except the guy that brutally smashed into our car. Strangely, I felt God in the car. I thought He had come to take us to His abode and I was fine with it, instead He had come to fill the car with his peace. It was warm and embracing. There was a gentleman who from a distance called in for E.M.S. to the scene of the accident. This man I later learned was at the event we did with the children. Arriving on the scene were two ambulances; one for Kendall and one for me. We were rushed to the trauma center at the McLeod Regional Medical Center. When the paramedics picked me up out of the torn car, my legs turned in the opposite direction. I remember saying, so that's what a broken leg looks like. On our trip to the hospital, one of the medics notified my children that we were on our way to the hospital. Maurice called Carolyn and she called our friend and sister of the faith Reverend Mazie who was a fully credentialed preacher. Not just to qualify her only by man's standards, but she is anointed and vested in the Holy Ghost to preach, teach and to bring comfort. She seemed to live the scripture found in Luke 4; certainly for me that night: The Spirit of the Lord is upon me, because he hath anointed me to preach the gospel to the poor; he hath sent me to heal the brokenhearted, to preach deliverance to the captives, and recovering of sight to the blind, to set at liberty them that are bruised.

I was somewhat comatose, but I could hear her speaking to my legs. She left her house to minister to my legs, when I couldn't do it. My legs were from the trauma, shaking like Jell-O. She spoke peace to my flesh, and health to my bones. She referred to my legs as a raging storm, but she began to insist, declare and decree that in the name of Jesus God quiet the storm in my legs. It was so amazing to hear and experience this thing. I had to go to surgery to get pins in my femurs for a straight healing in the bones. The nurses gave me a drug called morphine. I had this incredible hallucination or was it yet another open dream? I saw little men of armor jumping over my bed. I thought to myself; I must really be hallucinating, because men don't dress like that here. I felt God was watching me and holding me here for His service that only I could do.

Meanwhile, back in the intensive care unit of McLeod Regional Medical Center, Kendall was hanging on for his life. I remember vividly, my friend Gwendolyn say, "Louise, no matter what you see, Kendall looks good. Just keep that in your mind, Kendall really looks good. I was in a regular room in the hospital, and a tech came to take me to x-ray. I asked if we could stop by ICU. I needed to see my child. I was wheeled there on the stretcher after x-ray. I went in the room and there he was. I was not prepared! I don't care what was said to me, I WAS NOT PREPARED! He was bandage wrapped at his head and he had tubes everywhere. His favorite taped TV show was on the VCR, Lassie. I think this was an idea of his brothers, LaTonya and Mrs. Michaux. LaTonya is like a sister to my boys; Mrs. Michaux is Kendall's favorite teacher in the world. I touched him and he opened his eyes enough to let me see the burgundy color of his eyes. His tongue was protruding from his mouth. It was a sight that I could not handle. I told Kendall I would be back. At that moment I felt as if I was suffocating. The tech rolled me out and back to my room. Folk came to visit me, but I rejected all guests that day. I needed to be with God in the most urgent way. I didn't have time for pity, not even from myself, I didn't have time for chatter, or folly; I needed to reach God. I wasn't concerned about Why, Lord why? Just

Touch, Lord Touch! Restore my son back to himself, In Jesus Name.

The next day, I told Carolyn to get my newly recorded demo tape for Kendall to put in his ears. It had four songs on it that I had written, and Kendall loved those songs. WALK AFTER THE SPIRIT, WHAT SHALL SEPARATE US FROM THE LOVE OF JESUS, SINCE I MET YOU JESUS, AND WHAT ARE YOU WAITING FOR! I had an auto reverse, hand-held stereo recorder/player from AWAI. It played constantly in his ear, and Lassie, his favorite dog show was playing on the TV. Many prayers were heard on our behalf. Towards the end of the second week of Kendall being in a coma, Carl, Kendall's dad came in and said, "Boy, get up. You got people all upset. You gonna make it. Get up now." Guess what? Kendall woke up. He started his road to mend. Therapists of all sorts were working with Kendall. From the time he began to talk, he had a speech impediment. He stuttered. Three weeks after awaking from the ordeal of the coma, he did not stutter. However, he shook a lot. This was from being down so long from the coma and being on a ventilator to breathe for him. He also had a tracheotomy.

My mother had come from Charleston to take care of me, Kendall, and the boys. I was the first to arrive home from the hospital. Mommy was there being an intercessor, a nurse, homemaker, all the women of the world to me and the two older boys. I had a hospital bed to sleep in to help me in the healing process. The very next week on Friday, Kendall came home. CJ, LaTonya, Maurice and Carlisle went to pick him up. Momma was in the kitchen making collard greens, fried chicken, rice, gravy, and biscuits. We were so glad to see him. He was without the trach tube. Where the hole was in his neck, was a bandage. The doctors said it would close in a week or so, but he was fine.

We had a private dinner, just me and my boys and my momma. Well, Kendall went to the table and sat down. I was in my wheel chair; pulled up at the table and parked my chair. The other boys were already seated. Momma said, "Let's bless the food." Kendall, who did not stutter said, "Dog is dood and Dog is great. His words were indeed jumbled up, but he said, after being knocked unconscious, knocked into a coma, after being confronted with dying, and told the devil no, I will live and declare the works of the Lord, after having open head contusions, brain swelling, the doctors had to put his face back together; Kendall said, GOD IS GOOD, AND GOD IS GREAT! We went all the way in! The boys cried, I did my wheelchair dance rolling back and forth. Momma went running down the corridor of the house praising God for His goodness and His greatness! Lord, we had a sanctified dinner that day! Okay, that wasn't a dream, but you have to admit, you were blessed by how God truly intervened in this situation.

Chapter Seven
The Healing Wing

This is my third open dream or vision. I believe this would qualify as an open vision, because I was not asleep. The doctors call it hallucinations. It is described in the previous chapter as the men of armor jumping over my bed to protect me.

When I was young, I used to have migraine headaches very frequently. Sometimes I would imagine that I could put my head between two mattresses and someone could sit on my head and mash the pain out. In my mind, that seemed good enough to work. But, NOT! I could see my grandmother in my sleep praying for me when I would have them so bad. After I would awake, the pain would be subsided or gone. The mirage of my Grandmother was a blessing to me. I felt safe that she would visit me and pray. My mind remembered her sweet gentle touch and wonderful prayers. She had been dead since March 13, 1969. My grandmother could not come back here nor would she.

We are about to enter the dream and nothing prepared me for this experience. I had taken ill this day. I had a really bad headache, fever, and my body ached like no body's business. I was nauseated and having a hard time breathing. I prayed in the name of Jesus to take my sickness. It was almost too much to bear. I was praying then suddenly I am in the Spirit. I sensed a presence in the room like a thick fog and it was hovered over me. I was hidden and engulfed by it. I felt surrounded but not smothered. I have to admit I was curious about it but not leery by it. Then it seemed as if it entered my body, and the warmth of it was from my head to my feet. I could feel the weight as if it were sitting on me to press me in the bed. I cannot say that I was hurt by the pressure. It was an unusual experience, indeed. The light from the outside in the room was shaded by this presence. What seemed to be hours were actually a few moments according to the digital alarm clock on my night stand. The weight began to lift. I was trying to get a glimpse of what was happening to me. Then I saw it. From the right side of me, I saw the lifting of what appeared to be a wing. I could identify it as such because of the edge of the figure; it was feathered with a white bright glow underneath it. The wing was so large that it filled the room and dissipated the light as if someone covered the windows with thick drapery. The light that was seen was coming from the light under his feathers. I never saw the body or face that was attached to the wing, but when the wing was lifted, I was completely healed and restored to health; never having those symptoms again.

How excellent is thy loving kindness, O God! Therefore the children of men put their trust under the shadow of thy wings (Psalms 36:7). And, behold, the angel of the Lord came upon him, and a light shined in the prison: and he smote Peter on the side, and raised him up, saying, Arise up quickly. And his chains fell off from his hands (Acts 12:7).

Chapter Eight
Mother's Eternal Voyage

My legal (surrogate) mother went on to eternal rest on January 14, 1994. It was not hard to release her for she was ill a very long time. Her death was without lamentation; very peaceful. We all knew that she went to be with her God. Months later, I dreamed that I was at my daddy's house. My dad was asleep, and seemingly my mother was at work. She came driving up in their 1982 Park Avenue dressed in her regular work uniform; which was a gray pinstripe dress with her nametag. I was very excited to see her again because she had been gone for a really long time. I was yelling out for my daddy to get up and greet his beautiful bride whom he'd not seen for the same length of time. She was there in her house, in her living room. As he was collecting himself to greet her, she began to lie down on a revolving tomb like surface. My Daddy did not come immediately. Apparently he wanted to make himself as perfect as possible for their reunion, but I saw that she was being changed. Her dress changed. In a moment, a baby blue shroud draped her and her continence was illuminating in the room. It was the most beautiful sight to behold. I sensed peace in the room. My Daddy was ready to see his bride. While revolving on this tomb surface, Marie disappeared into the shroud and was taken up in the air like the rapture. My Dad and I begin to shout, dance and rejoice. It was her journey complete. God had shown us our loved

one's beauty; in her present state going to His presence –
alive unto Him. What a glorious state.

No matter how low you get, God's glory is come to bring
you peace and comfort. His glory will shine through when
there is submission. The color blue represents peace. The
tomb represents submission and the light represents the Spirit
of the righteous of God.

Chapter Nine
Daddy's Fallen Autumn

Tuesday morning, August 29, 1995 at around 5:45 AM, my dear Dad (adopted) died at home. The dream I had about him changed my life forever. It was a true healing of my mind and vexed spirit. I was present with my mother when she died, but I was home asleep this fateful Tuesday morning when I received a call that my father had fallen. I took care of my Father after my mother died; he was living with multiple myeloma, a cancer of the bone marrow. I had gone to Los Angeles, Ca. for the annual Gospel Music Workshop (GMWA). Two of my songs made its way to the new artist showcase and the new music guild. I was gone for 14 days. The day I returned, my best friend's son burned himself with gasoline on a fire. The day I left, her grandson was born. It is also the date of my parents' wedding anniversary; which is August 12. When I got back home, I caught up with my boys and went right over to help my father. My brother and dad would spend hours talking to each other, and my brother would help dad out a little as well. On Sunday night I cut his hair, massaged his feet; (he loved when I did that), helped bathe him, and made him comfortable. Monday morning, his sister came over to visit. My dad wanted me to buy him a small refrigerator, so he wouldn't have to leave his room for a drink or a cool snack. I did. Later on that day, hospice ordered a bed for my father so he could be at home, and it was delivered the same day. My father said something that was so bizarre, I thought he was delirious. He said, "Well tomorrow, all these things 'round here will be gone. Y'all gonna get rid of all this stuff 'round here." My aunt, his sister and I were trying to convince him that we couldn't possibly do such a thing. I thought he thought we might clean up the place and throw stuff away. But he knew what he was talking about. We were not to know. My father always said that when he got tired of living, his spirit would just leave his body. He would not have to suffer to die in his body. Well as I fore-mentioned, I got a strange call about 5:30 am Tuesday morning. I said hello. No response. Later on after the children had gone to school, my brother's wife called me to let me know that Daddy had fallen. Please come to the hospital. I called my daddy's sister and told her that my father was at the hospital for a fall. I went to pick her up, headed for McLeod RMC. When I got there, I was inquiring of my father's whereabouts. A person came toward me with lots of questions of her own, like who was I and did I care for him. I intelligently answered her probing questions, hoping she would hurry, so I could just see him. My Aunt came out of left field with her question asking, "Is my brother dead?" I already knew NO would be the answer. He simply fell, maybe breaking a limb. But to my surprise Karen, the social worker for the hospital, started to nod and shake her head replying, "Yes, I'm afraid so. I'm so sorry." That was the longest moment in the history of man. I saw and heard her say of my father's demise in slow motion. My aunt was as if air was let out of a balloon. She was out of control. I was calm (shocked). I hugged Karen, and said, "You mean my Dad's gone to be with the Lord?" She held me for a moment.

All I could say was, WOW, WOW, WOW! I couldn't believe he would leave me this way. I just knew I would have been with him to the end. I asked to see him. He was getting cold. His blue-ringed eye was showing, and he had a green carpet ball from the fall on his right cheek. I just rubbed his feet and head talking to him, releasing my joy that he was my Daddy, and thinking about how much I loved him and glad that I told him every time I wanted to, needed to. Karen let me stay as long as I wanted to. She commented that she had never seen anyone respond to death so calmly and that our bond must have been a special one; and it was.

As the weeks went by, it was harder for me to deal with the loss of my Father. He was my ABSOLUTE best friend! Now my best friend was with his wife and his heavenly Father and all of the family and friends that had gone on before him. I was left alone! I was happy for him. I was mad at him.

Chapter Ten
Two Copters

———∾∾∾———

This dream starts off with me waking my oldest son up to take me to the airport 3:00 in the morning. He said, "Momma, come on now! I've got to go to school in a few hours. Who are you going to see?" I was so sick with grief. I loathed the thought of revealing it, but in my embarrassment I said, "Maurice, you don't understand (stuttering out my explanation) I need to see my Daddy." "Ma, come on now. You know Granddaddy is dead. You've got to snap out of this." Maurice, I could tell was getting worried for me but there seemed to be nothing I could do. I was just too grief-stricken. I said to him, "YOU DON'T UNDERSTAND! Both of your parents are alive. Both of mine are gone! It really hurts. I miss my Daddy. I didn't get my last time with him. He left me in a hurry. I loved him so much!" I just began to pour out my heart hoping for empathy. "Now Momma," he said trying to console me with his tender voice and gentle caress, "We loved him too. You're not the only one going through. This is hard for all of us." He was right and I realized that, but I still needed to have my way. "So if you understand what I'm going through, you will take me. If not I shall go alone." Being the kind of person he was, he wouldn't allow me to journey alone. He sacrificed his sleep for a foolish woman's hope. As he was getting ready, he was murmuring in the background, 'my momma's losing it. Just help her. Lord, help me!' He drove me to the airport. I rushed into the building to get an unusual ticket that would take me out of the stratosphere. When I inquired of the woman, she looked at me in awe. I spoke quietly to her saying, "I am aware that if one could go to the moon, there must also be a way to travel to the planet Heaven. She responded by saying, "What you seek is not here, but I'll direct you to a place that will satisfy. We went further up the road through a dirt path fighting tree limbs and mud holes. It was obviously a present day jungle. I had finally arrived. Rushing out of the vehicle, I leave my son behind momentarily to speak to a man that would finally understand my plight. This man's physique caught me off guard. He and the establishment were unhygienic. The place was a pit mire; grungy and unkempt. The same man looked at me as if he hadn't had a visitor in years and was not ready to have any now.

He spoke in a very hoarse voice, "Yeah Lady, may I help ya"? Judging the man, I looked about wondering to myself how anyone this filthy with a place in even worse condition could possibly help me get to such a beautiful place. I had serious doubts. I was about to turn around and say forget this. Then it occurred to me to just give him a chance. After all, what could I lose? This was a struggle wondering if I had come to the wrong place, but my desire to see my Dad was far greater than my doubt. I questioned, "Do you have a plane that can carry me out of the stratosphere?" He answered quickly, "Ma'am, we got two copters. Way you bound? We got HELLicopters and then we got HEAVENcopters." "I'm going to see my Father. He's up in Glory." I spoke with such piety, "When can I leave and how much?" "Oh ain't nothing. Don't coss' ya nothing to go to hell, but coss' ya everything to go Over There. Whatcha got?" I said most assuredly that money was no object. He was very stern when he said, "Your money is no good for Heaven cuz you're gonna need more than money for this here trip. You gonna need blood, sweat and tears; even your very life." I was not expecting this answer. I was sure I would not be able to take the trip. I had not come prepared. The man saw my despair and told me to dig deep until it hurt, (he was talking about going deep inside my flesh). While digging deep, I was astonished to see what was actually coming out of me. Discouragements and doom were some things I saw, but then came triumphs and glory, visions with victories. The man took kindness from my heart, and gave me a pass to board this copter bound for the Planet Heaven. The aesthetic of the copter was lily white, but unlike any white on Earth. It was made of a sturdy type of foam-like cotton. Nothing like it has ever been witnessed with the natural eye. We started up. It was an all day trip, but it seemed like moments. At last I was there. I went up to the Great Gate of Gold. An Arch Angel stood there as a guard taller and more radiant than life. He inquired, "Who do you seek?" I answered saying, my dad, your Highness. He was a servant of the Most High, our Lord. He left without saying good-bye so I thought I might call upon him in his new abode. The angel asked his name, and I told him. The humongous Angel showed me where all the M's were. He gave me permission to seek him. He already knew I'd be back. I started the search for my dad. It seemed like several days in the M section, but my dad was nowhere to be found. I went back to the Angel and told him that I was unsuccessful. He suggested that I wait while he retrieved the record from the archives. When He returned he had the most fantastical book I'd ever seen. The book was as large as he. As he unraveled the ribbon attached to the life-size book and turned the pages he said, "Maybe he's listed under his heavenly name. (I believe he knew this from the onset, but perhaps I needed to experience the moment.) He continued flipping pages then he came across the name. He was indeed listed under a special heading, as one of the great faithful. I couldn't hear what the name was or understand the lettering of the Heaven's language because I was not yet transformed citizen. I implored the angel to give me the inscription. He did and I began the search for my daddy's mansion. I sighed with relief as I approached his new name and home. You talk about larger than life; my eyes were not prepared for the things I saw. The beauty! The splendor! My dad's estate was no different. I opened the door and yelped as I normally do. I was happy to finally arrive. I called out to him again. My voice resonated and echoed for minutes. I never even considered the thought of being in Heaven. I was focused on JUST SEEING MY DADDY! I was in Heaven, but with the consuming occupation of searching for Daddy. I didn't even take the time to glorify God that I was even there! I was in Heaven and after all that I had been through to get there, my Dad did not answer. Why, because he was not there – he was not there for me! If that didn't beat all! I thought to myself the cost involved in getting to this glorious place. I endured and suffered so much to find no Dad! I'm really pondering with him being a spirit now, he's like God, knowing everything in Heaven and Earth; I thought he should've known I'd be coming. It would mean the world to me to see him again and to say my proper hellos and goodbyes. My ego was sorely traumatized. I left like a spoiled six-year-old girl, in a bratty rage and heated rush. Storming from his residence, I went past the Archangel without a word, then hither to my son not uttering a word; who by now knew something had gone wrong. The ride back to Earth was challenged by the tense quiet. We are now back at home. From my personal embarrassment, I drew all curtains and blinds and shut off all lights to my house inside and out. I am quiet and motionless in my room when the phone rings. It was a member of my dad's church. She informed me there would be a program in a few weeks and I was invited to come participate in the program. Carrying over my hostility from my early morning trip, I was god-awful rude. I shouted, "I'm not coming to your ol' raggedy program! Nobody's gonna be there. Nobody IS there; nobody comes there!" The woman on the other side of the conversation said soft and easy, "Now Honey, don't say that. Anyway, it's a memorial service for your Father. He was such a dedicated member and he loved God and the church." I did become very humbled and embarrassed. I felt asinine and unworthy to attend. She thought grief had overtaken me. Her sincerity turned my heart as she included me the more. She forgave me without a thought. I asked who would be in attendance. She assured me that there would be family, friends, and dignitaries from every walk of life. Sam was the man, friend, father, and kinsman to me. I would, as any other person attending feel privileged to be a part. The week had come for the program. I went to the church with my music gear and started setting up. It was not obvious to others how annoyed I was when I thought of the condition of these people. Jesus is alive and they would rather spend their moments celebrating a dead man. Is this the worship that God is seeking? God is NOT dead – He is alive, but I'm here in a dead church celebrating a dead man.

In continuation of the dream, people began to gather at the church. When it seemed that everyone was in their respective places, the grand entrance was about to take place. There was movement, but no walking. The subject seemed to be floating in the air. It was the guest of honor. It was the exact figure of the man believed to be my Daddy. How could this be? He was buried! But there he was cold and stiff gradually opening his eyes. By the time he got to the seat he used to occupy, he was fully recovered or transformed as a living being. Some folk murmured while others shouted, "That's Brother Merritts." "Oh do you see? That's Brother Merritts!" "Oh my God, it's Deacon Merritts!" People were in great amazement and utter shock. So bizarre that no one would ever consider – It was a sight so unbelievable, I could hardly believe my own eyes. (No one knew what I had done just a few early mornings ago with the Heaven-copter ride to Heaven to see my Daddy's incarnated soul.) Suddenly, forgetting my own hypocrisy, I became intensely outraged. My fury was intensified because I went to see him and wasn't there. How dare he choose to show up to visit these people! None of them loved him or missed him more than me. Furthermore, my daddy knew my affliction and pain over his abrupt departure. I needed him to console me in a private and quiet place.

The hypocritical phase over people giving a DEAD MAN a celebration enraged me. It was dumb and I wanted out! I looked around to figure out why these people were tripping so hard about my Dad. He ain't Jesus! Maybe he was their new hero since their lives seemed to be over. Should I make the announcement that He's dead to me and to them? Well I made a determination that I would not talk to this ghost. I had already felt the rejection twice, it wasn't about to happen again. I felt before I would renounce him altogether that I would touch him and... I could touch him – but I would not let myself give in. I wanted to be gone. Directly following the memorial in honor of my father, people gathered at the Chase Street homestead. This was the place I knew so well as a child; so many memories. There were people and food galore and instantaneously, so was my Dad. He began to mingle and fellowship with his guests. I took courage to get my dad away from the crowd so we could talk. I needed him to know my feelings of his exodus. He was always a gentle man. He allowed me to say my peace. I went on and on until I satisfied my aching soul. He let me express myself without interruption. After pouring out my heart to him, he responded to me in a way that baffled me, "Is you done?" I was stunned into a shoulder hunching answer, 'I guess so.' He smiled and then said, "Well if you finished, 'den take my picture!" That was a strange request even though I am known as the personal paparazzi. I was totally mystified. "Hush up now. Gone over there and take my picture!" I couldn't believe my ears. After all the belly-aching and complaining I did, I would get this kind of statement: TAKE MY PICTURE! As awkward and strange as this request was, I followed through.

I needed to commemorate this moment forever. He posed in the living room over by the front door. I don't remember the expression on my father's face. I didn't expect any change in his face because he was walking dead. I was now satisfied. I had seen, touched, and I talked to my daddy. I went immediately to the superstore taking the canister of pictures to be developed. When the pictures were processed, what I saw in the photograph stupefied me greatly. I saw my Mother. She was standing beside my Dad in the photo. My Mother, who was the absolute love of my Father's life and his soul mate since 1934 was clutched close to her husband with the corners of her mouth turned up in a big smile. They were finally reunited after 21 months of separation. Sam and Marie were together on the photo. How did I miss that precious moment? They were together like old times. I was so consumed with my own grief of my Daddy being gone, I never considered my Father's happiness. I never considered my Mother. I was ashamed that I only considered me; me, it's all about me! My mother and my father were both my gifts. The photo reminded me of the precious gift they gave me called life.

The lesson of this dream seemed to be don't be so preoccupied with your gift or your ministry, until you miss God altogether. Keep your sights and attentions on Christ. He is the giver of good and perfect gifts. God will come, but we cannot expect His Spirit to dwell continually with us if we reject Him. He is a jealous God. Will you miss your opportunity to see Him, fellowship and commune with him? Gifts are not a substitution for God, but rather tools that God uses for His body to be edified, and for His good pleasure.

Matthew 6:33 says you seek the Kingdom of God FIRST, and His righteousness and the other things will be added unto you. (Finally, dead things can be resurrected. When all hope is lost and you can't get out of the pit, look to Jesus – He is the author and finisher of FAITH. Know the value of faith and use your confidence in GOD. He will get you out of the dead place and resurrect you to new life!

Chapter Eleven
Four Levels of Glory

———❦———

This dream was extremely beautiful. It was about a church with an unusual design. I had not seen this design any place before until my husband and I went to Florida as commissioned musicians for a Christian banquet in November of 2007. On our way to lodging, I saw a church that was close to the blueprint in my dream a few years earlier. I stopped to take a picture of this Florida church. It was eight sided with two stories, stain glass windows and doors, with a large parking lot, and buses in the church lot.

Here is a glimpse of my dream. I was going through my closet for the weekly offerings to the church. The pastor taught that all members should tithe on all of their increase and be a liberal giver of your substance. This is not restricted to money, but food, clothes, furniture, jewelry, or anything that you would use in your home. All tithes and monetary offerings were brought on the first day of the week and the first workday of the week all non-monetary gifts. So this Monday, I gathered some non-perishables and clothes to take to my church. When I got there, the appearance of my church had changed. It illuminated with such white fog like a glowing radiance. It was as if the sun was shining from the inside out. The structure was a four-story brick layout with blue stain glass and breath-taking beauty. I started toward the church to give my offerings. The first floor had some dressed tables with announcements and other information for the public and parishioners. The designated place to bring your offerings was on this floor. The challenging part of the floor was the offering area was unbearably hot. People were coming in and out bringing their gifts to the Lord's house. Those who came were drenched with perspiration. It looked as if they were the true givers and no matter how uncomfortable it was to them they met the responsibility. The occasional comers would complain of the heat and not return and encouraged other potential givers to stay away. I carried my gifts to its designated place and went to investigate further this beautiful building. I saw a golden elevator door on the first floor. As I proceeded to investigate this place, my eyes were indulged with the most magnificent sites. The elevator alone had a majestic atmosphere. The doors were golden in and out. The number indicator was positioned at the right side of the wall in a circle of crystal and gold. There were numbers 1 – 4 and the letters BH on the panel. No one seemed ever to press the "BH" button. Seemingly everyone knew that this was not a choice you would purposely make. The "BH" did not stand for basement hovel, but the "BOTTOMLESS HOLE". A smidgeon of heat could be felt in the elevator because it rested above the BH, but the ride between the floors was not unbearable. Pressing two on the number panel, I anticipated the opening of the door. When the door opened, I heard music. This was a floor for musicians, singers and other entities of ministry to perfect their craft. It was a holy place. One could sense the presence of the Lord immediately. I did even while seeing in my sleep. The structure of the edifice was eight sided to make for the corridors in circular formation. All rooms were occupied with different rehearsals. There seemed to be about 20 large rooms and four smaller rooms. I glanced in practically all of them and the minstrels were making beautiful music. In another room the ushers were dressed in attire and practiced their skill according to kindness and simultaneous walking. Yet another room, the educators of the Gospel were training from their Bible and notebooks. Everybody was working together for the common goal of ministry; the most beautiful sight to imagine. I hastened to the elevator for the third floor, and what a sight. The door to this room led to the sanctuary of God; the dwelling place of God and His people. There hung chandeliers like golden droplets of sun light and drops of crystal rain. The seating was dark wooded pews in a circular arrangement on the floor with red cushions. On the podium were enormous chairs that had matching tables. The sacred desk was designed in brick and stone. It reminded me of the brick and stone I imagined from the well at Samaria. I thought of the Living Water and the woman at the well. The colors and the furniture about the church reminded me of the "Old Rugged Cross". It was powerfully reverent. I immediately thought of the sacrifice of Christ. I was sad that one man had to suffer so greatly for a whole world. The stained glass was predominately blue with hints of gold and red. The "SON'S" presence seemed to be shining from the inside out of the sanctuary. An overwhelming sense of joy overtook me because Christ conquered death, hell and the grave and was living in me! There were people coming and going all the time, but never in disruption or distraction from true worshippers. There were people at the altar worshipping.

Some were walking while in prayer and praise. There were others in protracted prayer. Stringed instrumental music was heard in the atmosphere, but I couldn't tell from where. There were no wires for sound, nor were there any musicians playing. I tried to chase the sound. Was it coming from the walls? I put my ears to the walls, but the sound was clearly not in the walls. I placed my head to the floor. I was thinking that this music was coming from the musicians from the lower floor, but I was mistaken. There was no seepage of sound from the lower floor of musicians in rehearsal. This music was definitely coming from above. It was a pure sound of perfection. It was as if heavenly beings were orchestrating this sound. Oh, the presence of God was surely in this place. A thick vapor was evident in the air; I supposed it to be the cloud of glory. I stopped trying to find the sound and began to worship the Lord of my life. While in worship, I was looking around to allow my eyes to experience what my heart was feeling. Then a man sturdy but thin entered the room. He was wearing a robe, but not like the design of a preacher or songster's robe. It was not like the design of a dashiki, and it would be fair to say it was a strong cross between the three. The color of his garment was white with blue embroidery at the hem. The robe had a hood was about his head yet it didn't cover his face. You could also see his hair. The color of his flesh was the lightest color of brown, and his hair was a deep brownish red. His eyes were the color of Caribbean waters. This thin but sturdy frame's face had very pronounced cheekbones. His persona was so powerful, but meek. There was no denying who He was. He without speaking a word exuded humility and boldness. He looked almost frail, but you knew He was a powerful man. He was common, but when I tell you He was radiant, believe me, He had the GLOW!

His exuberance was enchanting and charismatic. At this moment my mind switched back and forth because under his arm He was holding a book. I thought to myself He must be a student of some kind. He appeared to be very studious. But if this is HE, would be a student of the book written about HIM? While pondering He came in dancing and spinning about. He was in great celebration. The bottom of his garment had an excess of material. As He danced and twirled, so did His robe. He danced all the way to the altar, then all around the sanctuary. Although He used no language, none could miss His open joyful display. Some folks did notice this enthusiastic worshipper and noted that it was indeed Jesus. Others worshipped greater by touching the bottom of his robe. Many more asked Him to touch them. There were quite a few people who noticed nothing at all. Even in the uproar of excitement, they maintained their stance of a worship look-a-like. They were not moved. The Bible says Take ye heed, watch and pray: for ye know not when the time is (Mark 13:33). Watching is a part of the participation and Worship imposters can't be moved into fellowship because their mood negates them from the relationship. The time was at that present when Jesus showed up to worship His Father, and He was excited to bless those who blessed them.

Don't be so engrossed with the look of praying that you don't watch in expectancy for what you desire. All spiritual blessings such as: anointing, fruits of the spirit, the ministry of reconciliation, the hunger and thirst to be filled of the Living Bread and Water of the Lord will be accomplished. Sensitivity of the Lord's presence is essential in gaining a real relationship. Relationship has a two way benefit. "My sheep hear my voice, and I know them, and they follow me" (John 10:27). Relationship is also vertical and horizontal; upward and outward. You cannot reach people until you have touched God and He has touched you back.

I took the elevator to the final floor; the fourth floor. It was a quiet floor. It looked like a business/administrative floor. Then it appeared to be more like a place of judgment. This corridor was plain in comparison to the character of the other floors. The floors were laid in gold bullion bars. It also had a peculiar ambiance. It was indeed a hallowed hall, and I definitely felt the reverence. I felt as if I had no authority to be on this floor because the time had not yet come so I left. My dream was completed.

The most awesome thing of the whole dream was I was close to the true worshipper our Lord and Savior. I saw the Lord being a true worshipper. He happily blessed His Father for THEY are one and Jesus blessed those who blessed Him. When the Lord and I commune, we are one. Christ is present to save, heal, set free and deliver...And the power of the Lord was present to heal them (Luke 5:17b). For the eyes of the LORD run to and fro throughout the whole earth, to show Himself strong in the behalf of them whose heart is perfect toward him (2 Chronicles 16:9).

Chapter Twelve
The Stairwell

———~~~———

Yet again I had a dream about traveling. By now I have sensed that from moving or traveling dreams, there are goals to reach and objectives to complete. This dream was definitely in that same category. I was going to a certain place in this dream. My legs were dressed with white stockings and white shoes. I thought it rather odd and eccentric since I never wear either. My head was also covered with a big floppy white hat. I was in a hurry to get wherever it was I had to go. I was carrying an infant child in a carrier. The child was close to me but I was not sure about the gender of the child or if I even bore the baby. The baby was also draped in white. The place looked familiar. We were in the midst of miniature store-front buildings and picturesque skyscrapers. I happened to pass a store-front edifice where people of God were assembled and praising God through singing, dancing and preaching. I was so moved by the worship that I wanted to go inside and praise. Looking on for a few moments, I talked myself into going inside. Although I took the time to go inside the storefront, this was not the assigned destination. I knew the urgency for where I was headed and was fixed to get a little spiritual inspiration before tackling this feat, but before I could make it inside the storefront, a dark, heavy cloud begin to fall on me. Moving away from the window to avoid a backlash from great winds and lightning, I ran in the street toward a deep blackened hollow space in the ground. The hole was so large that there was only one way across the street and it was through this black hole. I investigated any other possible options. When I got closer, I saw a stairwell. There was no apparent way around this hole except to enter downward into oblivion of steep deep darkness. As I made one step on the stairwell, my feet were drowned in the blackness. Fierce rain and winds came against me as I made my way down. I was so afraid to go down these stairs. The baby was blowing away from my hands. Even with a stronghold, I seem to be losing grip. Tears and fear overwhelmed me. People who were in the **store-front building came out to see me go down these very** steep and endless stairs but no one came to my rescue; they came only to look at my fate. The stairs appeared to have five sets. (Five is the number of grace) and about 20 tiny little blackened steep stairs. I crawled somehow to the fourth set of steps completely engrossed by my inabilities. Nearing the end of this set, maybe the last step, a woman appeared to me. She said, "Why are you crying?" I replied, "I was on my way to worship but I had to go through unfamiliar territory. I am afraid to go down these stairs. I cannot see my baby or where I am going. No one will help!" "Don't be afraid." said the woman. She had a peculiar glow about her. "But you don't understand, I said. "I don't really know where I am going, but I know I have a long way to go. It's dark and cold and unknown." She said as calmly as I was disturbed, "Just take thy baby to thy breast and go! Furthermore, look from whence you've come. See the little distance you have to your destiny!" She encouraged me to go. By the time I had gotten to the last step of the last set of stairs, the path was totally lit, and I commenced forward. Fear represents the enemy. Trust in the Lord with all your heart and lean not to your own understanding. In all thy ways acknowledge Him and He will direct thy path (Proverb 3:5, 6). The baby represents vision. Hold your dreams close and don't allow anyone to rob you of your dreams. The stairs represent perseverance to a new level of ministry. The winds and furious rains are the trials and tribulations in the world, but Christ said, "Be of good cheer, He has overcome the world." The person with the radiance and glow represents the Father of lights, in Him there is no variableness, neither shadow of turning (James 1:17). God was encouraging me to not be afraid. He was bidding me to come, so I went.

Chapter Thirteen
Little Becomes Much

———∽∽∼———

Another dream I had, was about my sons and me. We were to go to a familiar church. We came up in a limousine. There was sadness over the boys. They didn't feel right about going inside. I demanded that we go in. Upon entering, there were about eight people on the inside. My second son, Carlisle said, "Man nobody wants to go in this old dead church!" He seemed to take on a rebellion I had never known in him before. He went on and on; so much so until I said to him (in what I thought was a calm and quiet voice but it resonated to the uttermost parts of the world) "enough is enough!" My voice shook the Earth. People started to take notice of what I thought was spoken privately to my son. There were two tables in the midst of the sanctuary. One table was dressed in blue and the other table was dressed in white. As people came in, I invited them to come to the table and feast. On the white table, representing purity, there were crystal goblets and decanters with fruit aligning the table. On the blue dressed table representing the Holy Ghost was the heavenly character, the Commandments of God. There were plates of gold with baskets of bread loaves and a fresh harvest of fresh produce. As people started toward the tables to eat and drink the feast, the Lord began to spiritually and physically add to the church His body. There was nothing lacking in the room; food, drink, people and they were all on one accord. Considering the multitude that had come in; there was plenty of room. This little sanctuary where my kids had the disgruntlement grew the size of the largest dome ever visualized. It was heavenly! There were balconies filled with new and changed people. People were healed, set free and ready to hear! There was not a sound after the feast for all were waiting to hear the words of Jesus. There was a sign a true hunger amongst the crowd. They were listening for the voice of the Lord to speak a living word...and God spoke using me to deliver His message. I woke in a sweat and my pillow wet with tears. I was really overwhelmed by what I saw and how God moved on me. Luke 14:16, 17

Chapter Fourteen
The Other Side of the Street

Yet another dream one morning revealed a move to a city; seemingly very busy. It felt in a sense like San Francisco or New York. I was given a 9¼-inch high gloss gold key to fit any door on a floor of this grand apartment complex high rise. I was given privilege prior to arrival. Here I would reside. I was escorted by the man who gave me the key and clear directives. The key was to the housing complex's first three floors.   Unbeknownst to the grunginess of these levels, I was very excited to have my own place. The first floor had to be the worst of the worst housing I had ever seen or could ever imagine. The second was even filthier. As I graduated to the third floor, I was sick from the muck and decided I would not stay in such undesirable living conditions, (even if I had been given it free). I then thought, this is a very tall building, so the restrictions placed on me to choose from the first three floors seemed bizarre. I got on the elevator, pushed for the floor above three and when the door opened, I could hardly believe my eyes. I was in a heavenly place the entire floor was immaculate. The homes behind each door were the epitome of beauty and luxury. There were many vacancies. The key I held in my hand, trying to fit it to the previous halls, opened each keyhole. I tried every door. I saw a man I had known for a long time. We were from the same high school back home in South Carolina. I called him by his name, "Swilly, hi. Is that you? How are you?" He appeared startled to see me here in this place. He uttered, "Louise is that you? Man; The girl who was ALWAYS singing! Yep, singing ALL the time. I see you finally made it to the big time." I wondered from that statement what kind of place this was and if I would fit. I certainly didn't feel that I had arrived, to say the least. Swilly was an amazing character. He loved to match his clothes. I think his favorite colors were black, red and indigo. He had a certain pair of coveralls he loved to wear. He was well dressed, never wrinkled and always well groomed with a big shiny afro. His favorite thing to do was draw.

He had a skill to turn charcoal or pencil into a prolific piece of artwork that amazed teachers. His peers thought he was a deep individual and he was. There was not a person in our class more philosophical than he. I began to wonder why Swilly was here, so I asked. He told me he was there only as an advisor. Thereafter, a clone of himself came over to me and spoke a simple hello, but as if he knew me all the time. It was strange seeing two of the same people knowing they were not twins, and seeing them interact as different, as the same. The Swilly that had come into the conversation took me aside to talk with me; but not until he was given approval from his double who just nodded. It was agreeable. I didn't know my way around and his presence was very trusting and his company was quite enjoyable. I needed to go to the market as he supposed. The prophetic counsel that came out of him changed my life forever. I was being studied by the double. Swilly's double wanted to be certain that I could be trusted as well as trusting. He seemed compelled to warn me of danger. He said, "When you go to town you will run into a large number of mobsters a mile long. They will be standing on the street corner. You will witness badgering and abuse of women, men and children. You will see killings, but you must stay on the right side of the street. Carry on as you would normally. Don't faint, and don't lose heart. Stay focused; especially through all the friction and trouble. No matter what, DO NOT CROSS THE STREET! I will give you a map that will get you in and out of places without suspicion. I thanked him and started on my journey. Sure enough as I traveled toward the streets, there was the mob as he predicted. Hard looking men all shapes and sizes but all very handsome. They were each in their position using their tactics of aggression and abuse. Suddenly, I began to sing; not loud but with just enough volume to comfort myself and to ward off my fear of danger. My persona needed to feel unthreatening. We were very aware of each other. I walked with my head down continuing to sing until I was in the marketplace. I shopped many stores without disturbance. When I finished, I went back on the street, only this time I would be facing the left side of the mobsters. For a moment, it confounded me. I was not instructed what to do upon my exit of the building. I continued walking on the sidewalk originally walked. The unspeakable happened. The gang crossed to the side I was on. I was now remembering what the clone said, "DO NOT CROSS THE STREET!" I moved forward very slowly, apprehensively. I began to singing a little more boldly. This time unlike before, I held my head up to watch my would-be assailants. Nervousness was my closest companion. I thought I was at the end of my destiny, but as tense as I was, I looked the first man in the eye with the confidence of God while singing slightly stronger. When I was as close to him as I would be to my own thoughts, I stopped the melody for a brief moment, smiled, and never missed a beat in my steps. Impetuously, the first man nodded his head, and then held up his hand turning his palm to the gang behind him as to hold them from me. I walked completely through the crowd until finally out of sight, unharmed from the pack.

Preach the Gospel even if it's only a song or even when there are no words." These are the words that came to me after this dream. God is so awesome that He can use simple things to confound the wise. Again, He sends me forth. There is sin to conquer in the name of the Lord in the world, there are sinners to love. There will be spiritual warfare, but I am not left alone to fight, (Ephesians 6:23) the armor of the Lord is my proper attire. Danger will be in my path, but God's word lights my path, and He himself is my salvation, banner, shield and comfort. I will walk amidst the storm for HE is the calm peace of the storm. God is on my side. We abide together.

Chapter Fifteen
Lost Opportunity

———————∞∞∞———————

Isn't it funny when we are given tasks to do, we sometimes get the spirit of "get 'round to it." Just the other day, I told my youngest son to get me a cool drink from the refrigerator. On a regular he seeks to please my requests, but this day he was caught up with his own agenda and never got 'round to it. I got tired of waiting, so I got up to serve myself. The last of the soft drink Mountain Dew was left in the bottle, so without a glass, I helped myself to the remaining contents. I got the full benefit of that drink. Kendall could have had a share of it, but he chose to sit that one out, and it cost him soda pop with his dinner. Grant you, it was just a smidge, but the point remains if you are given a job to do, and you don't get it done, you will lose the rewards of that job.   I want to introduce you to the dreams of all dreams—a dream of lost opportunity. I TOTALLY missed God on this one.

One morning in 1997, I woke up from a dream that I thought was so far-fetched that I made the comment of how ridiculous it was for me to invent anything other than the familiar, babies, stories, and music. Now, when I see this thing practically everywhere I go, I get so sad and mad with myself. I missed the opportunity of a lifetime. More than before, I believe that God imparts bits of his knowledge and wisdom into a community of people and shows them witty inventions (Pro 8:12 KJ Version). – In wisdom dwells with prudence, and find out knowledge of witty inventions. Many people come up with the same invention, some act prudently, others procrastinate. Then there are those like myself who do not act at all. It is true that I have no right to pout at the *"could a, would a, should a,"* but what a loss of reward! My Pastor would often say the loss of reward is as eternal as the reward.

The dream started off with me building a vending machine. It was a very tall metal box with several slots and levers. I couldn't come up with a product that would fit the slots, so I gave the tall metal vending machine to my next door neighbor. I gave up any imagination about it, it was gone from my mind. Later in the dream I went to the movies and what I saw baffled me. I was at the counter getting popcorn from concessions. While glancing about, my eyes fell on the machine. As I drew closer, I saw the machine which resembled the one I let my neighbor have. It was indeed the very machine I gave to him. I read the contents of the vending machine. Playing back my secret thoughts I gulped. It made me wonder who would buy movies from a vending machine. That is the most ridiculous idea ever crafted. I began to laugh aloud. As people walked by, I looked in their direction asking the question, "Can you believe this, a vending machine with movies? What will they think of next? This is a non-brilliant idea, ha?" No one made any comments. Even the attendants at the movies were like me in the fact that the vision was not realized. I woke up from this dream thinking that was some dream, but who WOULD rent movies from a vending machine when we have all kinds of rental places. I let it go in my mind.

In 2001, I saw my dream come to pass at the grocery store. That's right; there was a vending machine with movies in it. I could not believe my eyes. The more I traveled the more I saw them in hotel lobbies, hospitals, grocery stores. I was flabbergasted! I always make the remark that I really missed God, when I ignored a witty invention, and to think, I used to pray for wisdom to give me witty inventions. What a lost opportunity!   God showed me the future, my future. I took this vision for granted by doing the "Sarah laughing at God," thing.

Sarah considered her own body being old and far from child bearing years. She secretly laughed at the idea of having a child because she was using her personal understanding, but what God promised shall come to pass.

I laughed at the idea of a future in the construction, production, and marketing of a movie vending operation, but like God showed, it still came to pass. It still happened without my involvement, except for an occasional purchase. It is most valuable to pay attention, to listen, research, and to take heed when God speaks.

I don't know the reason why I had this dream. Was it that I was supposed to create this invention or participate in some other type of involvement concerning this profitable idea? One thing is certain; I did away with the idea by mocking the dream and dismissing the thought all together.

Now in retrospect and regret, I realize I will never know what that experience would have yielded had I used my faith and imagination to go after what I saw. Who knows, I could have been one the richest women of my day. I know now that my act of procrastination is cast into the sea of lost opportunity, but then the Lord gave me a jolting revelation, "as often as you wake up with a brand new day, you still have the opportunity to accomplish what it is I gave you. No one else was given the specifics as I had laid out for you to see and do. Yes there are many vending machines with DVDs to rent, but I knew what I was doing when I assigned that vision also to YOUR hand. Just because you thought it was a dumb idea, I still expect it to come to pass by you. Remember the master who gave out the money for investment? I do expect a return. I will never repent for giving you a great idea."

When God told Abraham that he would be a father and that of many nations, it had to come to pass. No matter how long it took or the impatience to create his own plan from Hagar having his baby, it still didn't negate the promise God gave and it was the plan that would prosper. It was 13 years from the time God made the promise to Abraham and the moment it happened. Although there was another son Ishmael, he was not the child of promise. Even though Ishmael had blessings, Isaac was the appointed child of Abraham's seed, the child of promise.

These other video boxes are a fragment of the God's imagination too. They are blessed as in the case of Ishmael. However nothing takes the rank from his younger brother Isaac and nothing will take the place of the specifics of His witty invention spoken to me.

Chapter Sixteen
Who's Doing Your Job?

———∾∾∾———

After awaking from this dream, I shook and trembled. It made me get in a hurry. I was asleep next to my husband in a city in Florida. I awoke around 5:00 a.m. this March Friday morning to write down what I had just seen. The dream started with me getting ready for a musical presentation far off from home. I lived in a beautifully designed home. My favorite architectural structure was the view from my open bay window overlooking the Lake on the east side of the house and the center spiral staircase. Under the stairway to the left was a marble table that housed my keys, the phone, and the mail. As I was picking up the keys to leave the house, the phone rang. It was my old friend. It sounded like my friend and protégé Courtney. She was very excited to share some news with me. She asked if I would be coming over for a visit. "I have to tell you something that will astound you," she said. I said to her that I was on my way out of town, but I would stop by on my way out.

I got in my silver and red sports Lamborghini and headed to her house. I'll call her Courtney but I really did not know for sure who she was. Her spirit felt a lot like my god-child Courtney or, as I affectionately called her, Co-Co. When I got there, she greeted me. I don't believe we had seen each other for a really long time. We congregated at the bar with a spot of tea and tea cakes--our favorites. Her contemporary kitchen was an open space with a view of the blue green waters. Rushing through to get to the reason for coming, "So tell me this thing you were panting and raving about over the phone," I said. "OK girl. You are simply NOT going to believe this one. Well, you know how not into church and God and the bible I am. That stuff is okay for some people. I just didn't subscribe to that. I was living my life, enjoying my niceties and loving my world. One night about a year ago, I had the unquenchable urge to pick up a bible and read. HUH? Hold up; a Bible? Totally out of character for me, but the thought disrupted me so, I had to get up, go to a bookstore and buy a Bible and begin reading. Here is the shocker. I knew exactly what scriptures to turn to. I knew there was a Psalms 118. I had to read it aloud in its entirety. I closed the book and went to bed. I found myself up, reading that same text again, over and over."

"The more I recited, the more alive I became, the more alive it became. It was so profound, that it made me cry. Can you believe such a thing?" I said to her, "of course I could believe such a thing; all believers feel that very thing when confronted with the living word of God." I gazed at her. She had a different look; she had a glow. She was radiant, full of the life and the love of God. "Tell me more," I entreated. She replied, "I would wake up early in the morning or before going to bed at night with this insatiable appetite to read the Bible. When I went to work, I could barely wait for break time. I wanted to read this phenomenal book of prolific words. On this particular day when work was over, I left my car at work, and walked down to the northern cove, sat in the park and read until it was dark. I was so close to my house, I just walked home. I would never leave my car unattended and walk anywhere, but I had no anxieties. I felt like calm pretty waters, pretty much like the view from my home yet better. The feeling was quite amazing. The next morning as I was walking to work I saw, (and I'm sure it was there for years, but I never had the need to notice it) the cutest little chapel. I stopped in. The minister of the church was there. I told him of my experience. He told me that he was expecting me and he thought that I would never come. He said I looked far different from the person he was expecting. That was altogether a strange encounter. How would he know to expect anything from the likes of me? Why was any of this happening? But to take all of this in, I decided to leave my car in the garage and walk a few miles to work, just to walk the neighborhood of the beautiful chapel, thinking about my transformation, and the words of the Bible. I felt so at home coming and going there that I walked to work again and again, during lunch time and back again for my walk home. Then I wanted to attend the weekly meetings. The minister of the church was teaching the Bible. It was so amazing the things he said. It was almost as if God had written some of the text just for me. I could not get enough. I said to the minister, every time the door was open for a meeting, I would be there. I was a sponge; I devoured the Word which my soul.

I drove by the Chapel one Saturday morning. I noticed that there were a few cars on the grounds. I was not aware of any meetings or special services. I pulled in to see if I could get in on what was happening. Maybe I could be of assistance. I saw the Minister. After beckoning me, he said to me, "You are almost ready." I tried to process what he was saying. "I am almost ready; ready for what?" Courtney questioned. He did not explain his comment further. He just said that God is pleased with my assignment. There was an awkward silence she remembered. "I didn't know what to do with that. I went to this chapel day in and day out for about

388 days. This is the part that will absolutely blow your mind. Are you ready?" "Yes tell me," I shouted. I was completely engrossed in her experience.

Courtney continued, "Last Tuesday night as I was leaving the sanctuary the minister said, "I need to see you in my office." I followed him. The door was ajar. As he sat at the corner of his desk, he said I had been coming consistently for a little over a year; learning and soaking in all I heard about the love and the life of Jesus, the gospel of Jesus Christ and the Gospel that Jesus preached. Next Saturday at 3:00 pm, I want you to preach your first sermon." Co-Co swallowed a big gulp as my eyes stretched to the size of golf balls. I surely wasn't expecting that. Courtney said to me, "I know that today is Friday and this must be unusually short fused, but I want you to come hear me speak tomorrow. I completely value you as a Christian, a friend and I want your support. I know you will critique me. I don't know anything about anything like protocol, regulations or church codes. All I know are the wonderful things I have read, things I have been taught and what I have experienced since I discovered this new found joy." I never thought a day would come when Courtney and I would be having this conversation. Even though I had an engagement I needed to fulfill, I felt compelled to support her and to be a part of this grand phenomenon. I told her I would amend my schedule, and I would be there for her. As I was leaving, we saluted each other with a hug and kiss and I assured her that nothing would keep me away from this record making day. I got into my car. While I was buckling my seatbelt, I began to think. I might have gotten a little puffed up and a little envious. I thought about God and me, and my life long history of serving church, church people and God. When I cranked up my vehicle, I said under my breath, "How did that happen? I was always in church, serving, teaching, singing, and administrating. You never asked me to preach." Before the word was cool on my tongue, I heard down inside me, "I DID CALL YOU, BUT YOU WERE JUST TOO BUSY DOING CHURCH WORK. YOU SERVED WHOM IT WAS CONVENIENT AND YOU SERVED YOURSELF. YOU COULDN'T HEAR ME! I GAVE YOU COURTNEY TO BE A WITNESS TO, BUT YOU NEVER DISCUSSED ME. SHE WAS IN THE DARK ABOUT ME BECAUSE OF YOU. YOU NEVER TOLD ANYBODY ABOUT ME. YOUR LESSONS OF ME WERE GOD IS GOOD WHEN YOU GOT A NEW PIECE OF PROPERTY!" Wow! This was the time I sat up in the bed. I woke my husband and told him the dream. That was something to consider! I am doing all this stuff for people in the name of the Lord. Am I still in a season where God is trying to take me to new heights, new grounds, and new territories? Am I a light or am I darkness? Am I comfortable doing what I've already known? The Lord wants to advance me into new areas of ministry. He is bold. He is subtle. He is gentle. He is calling. He only says it once. This was the day I acknowledged the sacred call. I had so many excuses. I talk funny. He reminded me of Paul and Moses. They had challenges with speech, but Jesus overcame the world. Because he conquered, we are more than conquerors. I considered my contributing gift for the Kingdom would always be music and singing it, or writing it or teaching it, however our thoughts are not His thoughts nor are His ways like our ways. He knows from the beginning all things. His call is the most wonderful thing for your life, and it is your life's reward. One of the rewards is having a refreshed life into everlasting overflow, and the privilege to be with Jesus always, in life and in death. You be careful now. If you don't show up for work, the job you are meant to have, the boss will give it to someone else. They won't have your skill level, but they showed availability. It doesn't matter what you look like or how long you've been in a position. Longevity doesn't mean commitment by any stretch of the imagination. You could be in a thing just by habit and the passion is all gone and you're all dried up. This is for certain, if you do the man side and avail yourself, God will shonuff give you His ability. Don't let someone else do your job.

Chapter Seventeen
Vehicle to Destiny

Thursday is my husband and my day. I was born on a Thursday. Although Linton was born on Sunday, we met and married on a Thursday. This particular Thursday was no special day in June 2008. I stayed up too late the night before, so I overslept the following morning. I had a dream that shook me to the core. When I spoke to my husband who was away in Kentucky doing our usual job as musician on the road, he told me I should seek the Lord for His interpretation and council. I usually travel with my husband to the different places throughout the United States doing ministry and selling our inspirational music. This dream was about Kendall and me going on an excursion. I was asked to do a performance for a church in a different state. Kendall and I prepared for the excursion. When we got there, suddenly we were in the maze of a house. It felt like a funeral sitting-up or a wake. There were no familiar faces, but all were very nice and down-home people. Kendall and I had gobs of luggage. It appeared that he and I would be gone for a few seasons. Someone famous was to be in concert the next day and I was to join her on stage, but before that gig, I had to make a guest appearance for this church conference. Everyone that was at this house was making their way to the concert. No one knew that I would be there, they didn't even know me. Several moments went by and soon there was no one in the house except a very old lady dressed in black, and me. She said to me, "Way your lil' boy?" Shocked that she could be so observant in this house full of people, food and commotion, I said, "He's in the bathroom. It is his favorite past time, and his sanctuary." "Well y'all better hurry up, your ride gonna be here directly," she said. I was greatly amazed that she knew me, my son, or my purpose. Just like she said, an old beat up dark green pick-up truck with a gentleman who looked like a farmer came to pick us up. I referred to him as a farmer based on the cargo he had in his cab, crates of squash, corn, and eggs. Yellow has a couple of meanings one is happiness, joy, sunshine. It also has the meaning of cowardice and deceit.

The man (who didn't look familiar in or outside of my dream) stepped to the door, opened the door, came in and talked to us. The old lady left, and it was just him and me. He asked general questions, making small talk. I asked him, if he would be going to the concert, he replied no because he had to work, but he would be glad to give me a ride to the concert if I still wanted to go. I was stunned that he would do this thing for me. I said, "Sure." He helped Kendall and me with our luggage. We loaded the truck and headed to the next city. The farmer called himself Brother Mayer. He told me about his Pastor who was hosting the conference and that the pastor would take good care of me. Brother Mayer wanted me to give the pastor a message for him, "Just let Pastor know that I was already at the conference and that I brought you to the church." He explained to me that the Pastor already knew he would have to leave for work, but wanted to make sure Kendall and I got to our next destination without a hitch. He was getting us a Quick-Trolley. When the monotone Mr. Mayer gave explicit instructions for boarding the bus/train, he was precise in his expository. "There are two trains/buses. (The reason why I say bus/train in my mind it worked like both a train and a bus). Mr. Mayer went on to say "The first one will come in and wait for an extensive time. This is **NOT** the one you will ride. There is seldom anyone on that carrier. Take note; immediately after this one comes into the station, the other one comes – the Quick-Trolley; this train will only come in for a quick stop. Once you see the first train, make your way to the tracks urgently." He said, "You got a little time, but make sure you don't tarry." I went inside the station. I saw a lot of the saints that would be boarding the train with me. They were friendly and real sanctified. I bought some popcorn and a soda. Kendall wanted to do his usual bathroom ritual. I said to him, "Okay Kendall, we can't tarry around. The bus will be coming soon. Hurry up and come out or we will be left in this place. We don't know anyone here." He assured me with his two-thumbs up okay that he would be considerate. I finished my purchase and was headed outside where our baggage was. The first train came in. A lot of people got off to include the driver. He went for a soda, ice and a pack of snacks. The first train seemed as if it was waiting for about 40 minutes already. The driver went to ready the local motion for take-off. There were about three people on the train/bus. A little old lady with a satchel was trying to run to catch this bus. I heard them shout aloud; "Wait, here comes someone trying to board." All of them at once advocated for this petite and frail dark-skinned woman. The driver was very considerate. He waited as she slowed down to walk to the front of the bus. She was safely on the bus. Just at the time she was running to board that bus, the other bus I needed came up. There were many to board the Quick-Trolley. I looked around for Kendall. He was NOWHERE TO BE FOUND! I panicked! I began to call out to him while trying to judge if I should go after him. I saw that the line was still pretty long and the bathroom was just inside the terminal. As I began to go inside, I saw Kendall making his way to the trains; however, he as always was not in a hurry. In fact, he was lolly-gagging around on the dual bar slopes for handicap boarders. Kendall was pretending to have muscular dystrophy. I nervously yelled for him to get to me now! He stopped his mocking and came to me. I looked at the line, and it had shrunk greatly. I began to pick up my luggage and Kendall's. I directed him to come to me. These tasks were quite challenging. Then, without warning, Kendall turned in another direction. I yelled for him to come to me, while moving in his direction to coax him back to me. With all of the moving, coercing, trying to socially fit in, despite my aggravation, I dropped our luggage. Wow! What a feeling. There was no help for me. I gazed back at the line; it was less than fifty people seen in line. I made my way to Kendall, grabbed his hand, and pulled him and the heavy baggage to the end of the line. The last few folks were boarding the Quick-Trolley. I was desperately running, trying to make it on board. I heard people say, "You have two more running!" "Don't pull off yet, one more" "Hurry up!" I, with all the energy I could muster, yelled, "Wait for us!" "We're coming!" "Wait up, PLEASE!"

I was almost there. I was feeling safe, remembering the woman before me who boarded the first train after trying to climb aboard. Her strength was nowhere near mine and she got on! The train began to steam and the wheels started to slowly roll. I heard the tooting of the "chu-chu". The next thing I saw was the speedy jerk of the train. I stood in disbelief and utter shock. I couldn't believe what I was experiencing. I know the conductor heard me and the others speaking on our behalf! I bet he saw us!

I had to quickly recover and come up with a solution. I had to be on that train! I grabbed Kendall by his hand, and headed to the block ahead so that I could get on. It seemed at that time to be a bus. I was making headway. It was a brilliant idea. I was there! We had made it. I saw the bus turn onto the street where I was waiting. The bad thing was it immediately changed to the far left lane making it impossible for me to cross six lanes of traffic with baggage and Kendall. So I watch as the bus left me in a deserted land; unnerving to say the least. There were so many things I woke up feeling after that dream/nightmare.

Message #1 – Don't get bogged down with distractions. You can be led down a path to a place, that if you don't have discernment, you will be in total oblivion, wondering how you got there.

Message #2 – Kendall in this dream reminded me of things we face on a daily basis such as great opposition, and defiance. These things get us off track, and because we a creatures of "let me fix that for you Dear," or want to save the world, it distracts us from our true destiny. This nature causes loss of focus of what we are called to do.

Message #3 – Get rid of the baggage. The past should not have dominion over you. Let go of the sin that so easily beset you, and get free. RUN! Have patience! Once you let go, don't pick the baggage up again. Jesus said let burdens go. He offers his yoke which is easy and burdens light.

Message #4 – People stand around on purpose or they don't get involved because it's not their battle. They're not invested in your journey and are usually self-motivated to "just do them." This is not a kingdom mind-set; however there are many kingdom people who practice this behavior. The necessary thing to remember here is whether people are with you or not, whether they are for you or not, whether people jeer you or cheer you, you MUST STAY ON COURSE! You may have to make tough decisions to cut your closest allies. Jesus started off with just Himself, and then His circle grew to twelve, then to seventy. The day came when many people walked away, but that never changed His purpose. Stay in the game. Accomplish your tasks and gain your rewards.

Chapter Eighteen
The Cross

Wednesday morning October 1, 2008 I had this phenomenal dream just before the day broke. My husband and I were passing the Citadel of Hope Christian Ministries (CHCM) where we served. As we got closer to the church, we noticed people lined up in and out of cars, gawking. They all seemed awestruck. As we came up the rear on the right, we saw people looking puzzled at the building. When we drove closer, we were horrified because we saw the building's disfigurement. The cross that was built into the structure had now fallen from its position on the wall of the edifice. We got out of our vehicle in disbelief. As others looked on, my husband got out of the vehicle and watched as he pondered a plan to get the cross back up in its position on the outer wall. We noticed that the Lord's body had separated and had come off the cross. He was lying beside it as if He had been taken off the cross. The spike however was still in His feet. The position of His feet was left over right nailed together. Linton proceeded to the car for a sledge hammer. He then tried to fix the Lord on the marble cross. (Note: at CHCM, there is nothing but the cross on the exterior of the church's wall. However this completely stark, lily white body lay inches away from the cross. You would imagine that Jesus would be stone-like, just like the cross, but Jesus was human flesh). My spouse fashioned Christ back on the cross. In Linton's hand along with the sledge hammer was a spike he had also gotten from our trunk. My meek and unaggressive spouse was about to drive a spike with the hammer into the flesh of the Lord. He placed the spike at Jesus' right hand and with the hammer up in the air, he was about to strike into the right hand of the Christ (where there are pleasures evermore). Without even a flinch, the intense sound pronounced the agony as Linton struck the spike. I yelled out in great fear and trembling almost to the heartbeat of terror and panic, "What are you doing? What are you doing? You can't do this, oh my Lord!" As calmly as any human could be, Linton was the epitome of steel nerves. He replied back to me, "Darling, calm down. We are not repeating history here. This event has already happened. I'm not crucifying the Lord again; I'm just putting Him back on the cross for the world to see. He made another prick into the hand of the Lord. The blood from the first break of His flesh caused blood to gush from His hand and covered all who surrounded His body. The second blow was even more traumatic.

As I watched the blood in disbelief, I looked around and noticed onlookers were greatly affected by the blood of the Lord. In fact everything was covered in bright red blood dripping down and seeping through. There was a man who was walking with some others but he seemed to be disoriented and distorted; as if he were blind or lost. The others had their sight, but they appeared scattered and fumbling for the way. My husband and some helpers had solved the dilemma of how they might get the monument of the Cross back on the wall in view of onlookers.

These words came from my mouth as if were speaking on the Lord's behalf. The paradox here is that Jesus didn't speak up for Himself at His trial, before judges, or before His execution; with the exception of prayer to His Father. But this day, the righteous indignation says, "Hey whatchu doing? Do you know who I am? I am Jesus, Head of the Church!"

I woke up. There was revelation after revelation given after this peculiar vision. I called my husband who was away at the time and shared the dream and the revelation.

Message #1: Are you making light of your relationship with Christ? Do you even care about your worship and devotion to the Lord? Do you vex, insult, and dishonor the Lord with your lifestyle? Do you just apologize without any intentions of repenting and turning from that thing? You've got to change your thinking. You must decide to change your own mindset. God changes the heart or the spirit of man while you conform to His way of life. If we do not love the Lord, we hate Him. We are putting Him to open shame.

Rom 12:2 (KJV) And be not conformed to this world: but be ye transformed by the renewing of your mind, that ye may prove what is that good, and acceptable, and perfect, will of God.

Hebrews 6:6 - If they shall fall away, to renew them again unto repentance; seeing they crucify to themselves the Son of God afresh, and put him to an open shame.

Message #2: The Blood – The blood of Jesus was powerful enough to recompense the nature and deeds of sin for the entire world. Not all will receive His lavish act of love, however Jesus paid a debt far greater than we could ever realize. To think that one splatter of blood from the night He was beaten, abused, and rejected, nailed and hung on a tree, could return me back to Him is an awe-striking thought. In the dream one splash covered all who were in proximity and those nowhere near the vicinity. Even though everyone was covered by the blood, there was one who remained blind. He was going in a different direction. God calls us all to accept a pure and holistic lifestyle. There are the blatant that will refuse this way. Are you one of these people?

And the blood shall be to you for a token upon the houses where ye are: and when I see the blood, I will pass over you, and the plague shall not be upon you to destroy you, when I smite the land of Egypt. Exodus 12:13 (ASV)

The devil is the plague that seeks to destroy you. The Blood is the token for your covering and safety. Don't go in an opposite direction. Don't be blinded by the devil's devises. 2 Corinthians 4:4 – In whom the god of this world hath blinded the minds of them which believe not, lest the light of the glorious gospel of Christ, who is the image of God, should shine unto them.

Also, in the presence of the blood, were people healed. This still holds true today. Jesus the same yesterday, today and forever!

Hebrews 9:12, 28 – Neither by the blood of goats and calves, but by his own blood he entered in once into the holy place, having obtained eternal redemption for us. 28 So Christ was once offered to bear the sins of many; and unto them that look for him shall he appear the second time without sin unto salvation.

Message #3: The church has removed or substituted the blood and the Cross for carnal things rather than the spiritual things which got us to Christ to begin with. Fine facilities are fine and wonderful, but if we are not bringing people to the point of Calvary where life ends and begins, there is no need for the sanctuary. If we are not provoking people to righteousness, what is the point of the Gospel message? If we are more concerned about the mood of people rather than the move of God, we are sadly indicted. Take hold boys and girls, ladies and gentlemen! Stop making excuses for your wrong. The Lord is NOT amused. He will reserve your right to live in your broken state all the way to the day of fire and brimstone. You already know what is right and what is wrong because of your first brother Adam. The second Adam, Jesus has come with explicit instructions to live forever with peace, joy and all that is good. Preachers, PREACH CHRIST and not your own agendas and schemes. LAYMEN, LIVE FOR GOD! That alone will draw true seeker to God.

Chapter Nineteen
Hospitality

Very recently, my husband, son and I were living on the west side of town in a drab apartment with not a lot of light or color. Although I made it a cozy quarter, it was very timid in space. For the most part it sat in a pretty nice residential area, but with us not being used to living in a duplex, it was a little different and quite challenging.

We were reduced to this quaint duplex because our home was in foreclosure. The saddest detail was not just one foreclosure but two; two cars were repossessed within a year. All we had was GOD. Linton and I were not in a good place emotionally, naturally or spiritually. It was probably one of the roughest seasons we had experienced as a blended family.

Kendall was undaunted by life. He was not worried about anything. His innocent and protective state kept him oblivious from our life struggles. Steady talks were about his big plans of parties for dogs and wrestlers.

Life and our small space were caving in on us. Let me tell you, a tight space will let you know how much you love your family members and how much you love GOD. As an example to the petite character of my apartment; the kitchen was so small, I had to go in the living room to think of what I was going to cook for dinner. We were always bumping into each other's personal spaces.

I needed relief from the economic deprivation, liberty from the smothering clutter and way out from the stifling of space. Sometime in January 2011, I landed a job through an agency ministering in the town of Chapin to a woman who had mental illness. She called me "her nurse". I felt honored because back in the day, if you were called a nurse, that meant you had a noble and reputable profession. To be named a nurse meant something, whether you went to school for it or not; it's a ministry – it is a calling. I loved working for her because it was like ministering to GOD. I did it as if she were HE. To accept Jesus' ways is to accept His love and to accept His love is to receive His ministry of hospitality. More folk than few who were in the field of nursing dressed the part and served the part. However in comparison today, it's not the same. Now don't get me wrong, there is still a great deal of people who care with Godly compassion.

I had a real experience of good nursing when I was in the North East Hospital in 2013 for symptoms of a stroke. This affliction came over me while I was in rehearsal preparing for a church function. Linton, James, JoAnn, Dee and I were getting some ideas together for an upcoming function. We were about 40 minutes in when suddenly, a pain like never before gripped my head. It was so sharp that I went down, then another, then another, by that time I couldn't speak, I was going limp.

My husband and James the gentle giant picked me up and carried me to the car. The hospital was just moments up the road and it took no time to get there. They rushed me in passed all who were already seated to be served in the waiting room. I was taken to this cold and very brightly lit room and there were so many medical personnel rushing and caring for me. They asked questions as they attempted to assist me. I felt greatly overwhelmed. They could not get a vain to apply an IV. After several failed attempts they finally got an IV in. They took me up for a scan, they were certain I had a stroke. There was no evidence of a clot or bleeding out, but the doctor advised my husband of a shot that would thin my blood and stop any clots. The shot had to be administered within the first three to four hours of the stroke to be effective and we were on the precipice of time.

The doctor came in to share the fear factor: 30% of the people that had the medicine were not affected, 12% got worse, 3% got better and 3% died. Linton was not willing to make that kind of decision with such high risks and low results. Linton, Bishop & the Saints began to pray! I became a patient of the hospital. The next morning, I had more extensive tests done that proved I had two prior strokes before this one, but with no visible damage. Now I have outward appearance of a stroke but no brain evidence of a stroke.

My left side had no feeling. A circulation devise was placed on my legs to massage then to keep even blood flow. The blood pressure readings were out of control the night before. I was put on a blood thinner and a blood pressure medicine to control these levels. I thought that if I changed my hospital environment, I could be back to my natural self. Wouldn't you know it, while I was in the hospital I became non responsive because of a seizure. Straight to the IC Unit I went for about a week. After my release back to the regular floor, they prepared me for discharge to a live in rehabilitation center.

This Rehab Center is nothing short of a fancy resort on the NE side of the city. Their entrance and lobby are breath-taking. They house four restaurants, a movie theater, a library, sport's bar, a coffee shop, a meeting room and a beauty salon and many more amenities. It is an immaculate place and the staff and nursing facility is top notch.

Everyone I met is not only professional, but human, kind and caring. I am sure I had the best staff in all of South Carolina. To help me get back on my feet, I had trainers and therapists who understood my injuries and pushed me slightly beyond my ability until I reached my full potential. I had three of the best in Physical Therapist, Occupational Therapist, and Speech Pathologist. It was an awesome work of training and will power.

Then there were all of the well-wishers and family members who came by to pray or to bring gifts and things that would make me happy while I come back to wholeness. Anyone who knows me personally knows I absolutely love berries. People from far and near were bringing me gum, juices, berries and chocolates and let's not forget about CHICKEN and tea. There were a few who cooked American food, Jamaican food, and Soul food for my family while I was on the mend. When people take time to visit and touch you that means a lot. There is NOTHING more power than love. A touch, a smile, a kind word or gesture comes from love.

I have a personal aid that was like none other. No matter what, she was there to make sure I was not left behind or left out. This woman made certain that the slightest need I had was met. I had that in my two earth angels JoAnn and Aliyeah. My husband and the staff loved JoAnn especially because she went beyond my personal care to help them. When she would make my bed it would be so inviting, I wanted to get in, but then this big pause would take over because it was too attractive to mess up.

God sees and remembers every day you are kind and compassionate to someone. In order to be a people person, you must have people skills. In order to have people skills, you must have GOD. He is the only one who can give us the ministry of hospitality.   In the book of Romans, chapter 12 the ministry of hospitality is dealt with. Essentially, we are not to follow after the world's ideas, present our body to God, prefer others over ourselves and not to think we're better than any other person. We will all experience caring for someone, whether it's a child, parent, friend, spouse, neighbor, or in a professional manner. Remember Jesus said in Matt 25:40[b] Inasmuch as ye have done it unto one of the least of these my brethren, ye have done it unto me.

Mary Magdalene understood the value of ministry. She sowed her tears for the comfort of a Divine man headed to His death for the entire world. Jesus understood the ministry of hospitality in so much that He found the sick and the poor to encourage them and to bless them. Sick people, poor people and mentally ill people are usually those abused, taken advantage of or even forgotten. God wants us to remember what it feels like to be rejected. According to Isaiah 53:3 He is despised and rejected of men; a man of sorrows, and acquainted with grief. If anybody knows how rejection feels, it is Jesus. We too know the sting of rejection, and it does not feel good.   The good news is we can be healed from the wounds of rejection, being forgotten and abuse.

Whether you are a nurse with papers or not, helping someone along your journey is a wonderful and noble ministry. My Dad used to say, "A dog deserves the time of day, and it's just nice to be nice." You don't have to be a minister with a license to do ministry. Jesus didn't have papers to be a preacher but He changed lives and we're still talking about Him today! Say to your own self: what kind of changes am I making in others' lives? One thing is for sure, you won't make an impact in someone else's life until you make a change in your own.

Chapter Twenty
Restoration

—–∿∿∿—–

There's a song that was written well before Hezekiah Walker ever made it popular <u>Lord I'm Running Trying to Make 100 because 99 ½ Just Won't Do.</u> Well in this life, there are goals to achieve. Ecclesiastes 9:11 says I returned, and saw under the sun, that the race *is* not to the swift, nor the battle to the strong, neither yet bread to the wise, nor yet riches to men of understanding, nor yet favour to men of skill; but time and chance happeneth to them all. (KJV) You don't have to be the fastest, you just have to finish. As Matthew 24:13 says "But he that shall endure unto the end, the same shall be saved." Here's the question, do you have to be in EVERY race? Go to EVERY meeting? Do you have to do everything? The answer is emphatically, unequivocally, absolutely, positively undeniably NO! There is something in the English language that is helpful to the human race and that word is called REST. Webster Dictionary defines rest as a noun – stopping work or activity, sleep, a break, relaxation, respite.

Jesus was the most popular man that ever walked the face of the earth. (KJV) Mat 4:23 And Jesus went about all Galilee, teaching in their synagogues, and preaching the gospel of the kingdom, and healing all manner of sickness and all manner of disease among the people.
(KJV) Act 10:38 How God anointed Jesus of Nazareth with the Holy Ghost and with power: who went about doing good, and healing all that were oppressed of the devil; for God was with him. One example, the Lord Christ needed to take a break from the crowd in Mark's account after feeding five

thousand men. Think about that! That's a lot. First He's preaching then He turns around and feeds the people. Right afterwards, He sent His disciples to the boat so He could escape to pray.

Jesus was so in demand that after multitudes of people came to hear His words, He wanted to go to the serine waters. He said, "Let us pass over unto the other side." While Jesus was trying to catch a nap in the boat, fear caused the disciples to wake up the Lord. Based on His answer, He was annoyed! "I'm okay – you're okay; we're ALL ok. But I'm trying to sleep here. You're all with me so why is it that you have no faith?"

The point of this paraphrased conversation is that everybody needs rest! GOD is infinite and immutable, but after putting all He had in to the making of the earth and Heaven and everything that do dwell, He rested on the seventh day! We can't do it all. My Daddy used to say, "If you don't care for your body, your body will kick you out!" another famous saying of my Father was, "YOU WORK THE JOB, DON'T LET THE JOB WORK YOU!" The highest form of worship is not hallelujah, but it is lifestyle. You must make important life choices to have good success. What is the point of going and going and going and going, then when you're really needed for what God calls important, you can't because you're too spent. From my dad's famous words, "Your foot is on the gas. You know how fast you ought to go."

Now this is by no means a license to do NOTHING! However you must pace yourself in order to accomplish the large scope of things. It's not ALL about you. GOD first, and then the company you've been placed in to accomplish what you have been designed to do. Play your role and be good at it!

There have been people who have not kept their body and the next thing you hear, they're dead. And you say, man he or she died too young! We must take care of our temple, or we'll die prematurely. You may be in that number of ignoring your body right now. I was definitely in that number and was about to be named among those that died too soon. A stroke or heart attack is something, that if GOD doesn't intervene, you will die from. I was away from my house for a great deal of time because I failed to REST. Take time, recover, and retreat. Get my Drift? There are only 24 hours in a day. I need to sleep at least 7 or 8 hours a day, but I worked days and nights plus ran a household, took care of a special needs son, did outside ministry, along with church! In retrospect I realized that only GOD could have kept me from something that is deadly to us all. But the true lesson in this is TAKE CARE OF YOUR TEMPLE!

For all of the Bible scholars, I know you may say this text is taken out of context, but take this up with the Lord – He taught me this very recently. (KJV) 1Co 6:19, 20 What? Know ye not that your body is the temple of the Holy Ghost *which is* in you, which ye have of God, and ye are not your own? For ye are bought with a price: therefore glorify God in your body, and in your spirit, which are God's.

The sweet loving personal Christ gave value back to me when He said, "Weesy, I gave you some assignments, some attributes, I separated you and I bought you with a price. You are mine. Glorify me by doing my will without over doing it. Works won't get you in ME, but overworking will get you to ME." HE also told me to give myself the ministry of QUIET. "I need to hear the sound of NOTHING and DO NOTHING!" I get it Lord Jesus. I say yes and AMEN.

David understood the importance of solace and rest. He went to the still waters to be refreshed, restored and forgiven or set free. There are many facets to the human being; spiritual, natural, physical, physiological, mental, emotional, sexual, and psychological, to name a few. GOD put in all of us His natural healing power. Just think about that cut you once had on your finger. Now there's no sign of it; that was God's healing agent inside your human body to restore you back to your original health. But there is a healing anointing that is spiritual that will touch you at the point of your hurts in all areas. My Bishop says often, "Don't focus on your crisis but focus on Christ that is willing to deliver you. Faith and love are the most powerful elements in the universe. Moreover, nothing is more powerful in the healing process than love, forgiveness, hospitality, and rest. Lord, thank you for healing my body quickly from the effects of a stroke.

The Bible defines rest a little differently. There are three prospective of rest. The first: Sin beats up and tires man out so Christ tells man to rest from the burden of sin. Come and learn of His ways and you can have rest for your soul. (Matthew 11:29-30) The second: The Lord enjoys where He dwells on the right hand of the Father. Christ finished the work so that we could enjoy His eternal rest. (Hebrews 4:10) Finally faith works, therefore we rest in faith internally. (Mark 11:22) Have faith in GOD that HE will take your burdens and solve your problems. Be bold and ask GOD for grace and favor. Having those attributes of GOD will relax you, comfort you and remove the burden of duress and stress.

Chapter Twenty-one
The Plan – Die-2-it

———— ∾ ————

I was very unhappy about my figure. I didn't buy clothes because I didn't like the feeling of failure or struggle just to try on a garment. I would make mention to my spouse to help me with a fitness plan. We would start off great but at the first sign of pain I would recant. After a walk in my neighborhood one morning, I came back home, sat on the couch and fell into a deep sleep. What I saw in my dream was quite amazing. My imagination took me on an experience; that if I follow what I saw, my life would've change completely. I dreamt about a room that was dark, cold without color and decorum. It was absent of everything representative of smell, light, warmth. It had only a smidgen of air, and that was the oxygen scarcely in me. I wasn't afraid, because I could sense in my space a serene and tranquil feeling. I could hear a distinct sound, personal and engaging. There was no proof of a door, but clearly the sound was convincingly the rapping on a door. I didn't try to discover its direction or investigate further because, if I was not already familiar with my own looks, I would have forgotten my own form. It was pitch black and all I saw was the darkness. As my perched body occupied a small space of the room, my mouth answered the knock, "I'm in here." There was no sound of a door opening with a squeak or creak not even the closing with a thump. Instead was the change of the room from black, dark, mundane, to illuminative, brightness with whiteness, grandeur and LIFE! The LIGHT had form, a body even. I surrendered this thought that I may be in the company of Reverence, but how could this be, in view that no one can see God and live from the Old Testimony's script. However, here I am with a divine sculpture; the image or the REAL DEAL of the DIVINE PRESENCE; following sanctity, sanity, peace, and calmness. Everything was now new, open and filled with THE LIGHT. One would think that in the midst of such deity, there would be such a reverential fear or awe; and indeed it was all of that, but it was much more than that. It was like kinship, comradely, close friendship. GOD felt pleasant and full of joy, unmatched by my feeling of hope and serenity. He felt like my parents, my spouse and my children all at once. The emotion was quite overwhelming. God is in my presence and I am embarrassed by my presentation. I'm thinking about the scripture now, Present your body, wholly (completely), holy (reverently) and acceptable. I didn't feel whole, holy, or accepted. I was sad about how my body had become, and He said, "I will help you with your achievements. First, what are your plans?" "Well", I said "I don't really have a plan, but I know I need to do something." He placed His glorious hand on my left sluggish shoulder and said, "If you want to be made whole, this is your regimen from now on.

First, when you get up early in the morning before you start your day, you must PRAY! I only want you to pray in adoration and exhortation. Pray MY WORD, pray with your heavenly language then listen. This will build you up in the

Holy Ghost and your most holy faith. I need you to take deep inhalations and exhalations. All together this should take no longer than 60 minutes. Next, be active at your own dwelling place with stretching out your muscles then leave your house walking or running. I want you to be aggressive. If you don't suffer, you won't reign. You need to reign over your body. Your body is subject to you. It obeys your recreated spirit; not the other way around.

The first week, I ONLY want you to eat foods that have the colors green, and yellow. Second week, red and green, Third week, Orange and brown, Fourth week fast no meats or sweets, fifth week, white and black but no rice or starchy foods or sugars and the sixth week, Beans ONLY no meats. Drink only water all during the day and antioxidants juices. Then I want you to clean your bowels with a tea. Follow suit for 40 days. 40 days is six weeks. Six o'clock begins a new day. DO NOT eat after this time. If you are hungry, drink or chew a gum. Fast until morning. Follow my instructions. Always eat smart and small. Stay the course! You can do this!" He began to encourage me that with Him ALL THINGS ARE POSSIBLE! I must participate with Him and cooperate with Him for a sure victory.   It was over. I woke up from the dream thinking WOW that was sooooo real. When my Honey got home, I told him of the dream. I was all animated but he was in his usual quiet demeanor. I'm nudging to get a response from what I thought was amazing event of a dream. He said somewhat quietly something that he has spoken about before, Well Darling, if you don't like what you see, change it!" These are the famous words of my husband.

My encounter with my Spirit this morning was preparing me for change. I have had varying kinds of hurts all of my life, so I had succumbed to the idea that I am not going to inflict myself with pain. However the truth of the matter is, if I don't get the victory over pain, it will overtake me, and my body will die from a lack of usage. I am not afraid of pain, I just don't like it. But hey, I'm a woman! I've had natural childbirth, broken femur, popped Achilles tendon, ripped cartridge, trapezia muscle tear, migraine headaches, backaches, seizures and a stroke. And that's just some of the physical trauma I've endured, which doesn't embrace the emotional, and mental hurts I have suffered.

If I can have faith in God for emotional and physical healing, then I can have faith in God for the restoration of my body. I have to face the fact that sooner or later I will reap whatever I have sown. In order to change I must endorse and follow the plan! I've got to diet or in other words DIE TO IT (PAIN). There will be pain now or later, but if I stay the course, and yield to the work, I will gain health.

Twenty – Two
Journey Onward to Purpose

The path is not obscure. Your destiny is sweet and the journey you take awaits you. Every human being is born to accomplish his life. How we live out our lives is contingent on the choices we make. Before we would ever pick up and read any line in the Holy Writ, we will discover through life that there is good and evil, happy and sad, right and wrong, etc. I believe we all want to choose the good for the most part.

The Bible is specific when it points out that there are blessings and curses, honor and dishonor, life and death and that every choice we make is up to us via our own will. In a familiar passage of the Scriptures, it says ...that I have set before you life and death, blessing and cursing: therefore choose life; that both thou and thy seed may live (Deut. 30:19b). God totally wants us to choose life, but it is sad to know that some will choose death. We all will live or die by the decisions we make.

I believe God places His design and purpose in us before we are born, and when we are children, we become acquainted with those designs and plans. Moreover, we begin to practice them in our play. We get that sense as it becomes more familiar as we practice during playtime. In my case, I was practicing what I would do for life. Role play was fun as I imitated being a mommy or teacher or preacher. Even as adults there are people that influence us. We keep the things we see in people that fit us, and discard the things that don't.

A job is something you do to get earnings. A vocation is what you are meant to do. It is the drive or the passion of your life. Two of my sons have entrepreneur spirits. One owns a recording studio and record company. He eats, sleeps, and works his vocation. Another son dreams of someday making his dream a reality while another son plans daily on his fantasies. Two of the boys dream of their path, talk about their path to become. The difference in the three is one works for a living, the second lives for his work, and the last dreams of becoming great without knowing how to work a solid plan.

Pursue your dream. At the planning stage, you don't need money until you need money. All you need is a plan and a will to get it done. God gave each person an imagination so He could dwell there and for us to live out what was placed in us from the beginning. Imagination alone will not get you to your destiny, but planning and work will.

I had challenges with dyslexia as a child, but it didn't stop me from writing. Let no challenge stop you. Sickness is a challenge, so are low self-esteem, poverty, and the environment. But, like Paul who wrote "none of these things move me" (Acts 20:24). You won't be perfect. Practice not for perfection, but for excellence. You will have the help of the Perfect One, who will mature your works.

Before the foundation of the world was formed, we were predestinated. This is proven in Gen 1:28, And God blessed them, and God said unto them, Be fruitful, and multiply, and replenish the earth, and subdue it: and have dominion over the fish of the sea, and over the fowl of the air, and over every living thing that moveth upon the earth.(KJV) This is the natural portion of man. The spiritual portion of man is the proven in Luke 10:27, And he answering said, Thou shalt love the Lord thy God with all thy heart, and with all thy soul, and with all thy strength, and with all thy mind; and thy neighbor as thyself.

Don't get the wrong idea about it; we are all destined for greatness, but it is by our own will to accomplish. I did make an assumption for many, many years that my platform or pulpit was the piano bench, piano and some words I wrote in a song for a thought provoking message. It had its instance, its purpose and its power.

There were many obstacles in my life, starting at the time I was conceived: I was given over to adoption, I was loved, despised, envied, mocked, and persecuted. Sounds like anyone you know? I dealt with my own demons like mental illness, sickness and disease, depression, stress, doubt, fear, worry, suicide, promiscuity, adultery, kleptomania, sexual indecision and countless other thoughts and deeds, OH, BUT GOD! Trust me when I tell you I had lots of opportunity to give up and say forget this, I'm out! I can't get it right – why would You even call me – why would You want me – I'm so raggedy – all the questions one would ask if they couldn't find their self-worth.

I tried to commit suicide a few times as a teen and got rejected; thank God! There were times when I was comfortable in knowing I was doing what I loved to do and that it was what I was supposed to be doing. Nonetheless, when opposition came to break my spirit, I became uncomfortable. I have had days when strong family members would say you can make it, then in the same day other family members, for whatever reason, would say, "You're nothing and you'll never be anything. You're ugly and you'll never be good for nothing. You think you pretty? Well you ain't! You ugly! People don't even like you and if they did, they only like you because you can sing, and you can't even sing that well." Then, while in church, I'd listen to the different people who say that God is a present help, in the time of trouble, He'll hide you. The songs lifted in church said, JUST AS I AM, WHERE HE LEAD ME I WILL FOLLOW, NO NEVER ALONE, WE WILL UNDERSTAND IT BETTER BY AND BY, FAIREST LORD JESUS, YES, JESUS LOVES ME, AND JESUS WANTS ME FOR A SUNBEAM. Man, if you want to talk about confusion, all of this information left me in a conundrum. I could have chosen to go in a different way, but somehow, I was propelled into a family where the members loved God and the great lessons I learned (through unorthodox methods) taught me things such as humility, patience, kindness, compassion and integrity. The price I paid for these lessons is immeasurable. These are all the characteristics of the Lord. Now isn't that amazing.

Understand that God has already done what He's going to do in our lives and the enemy is actively trying to sabotage the plan. You are made wonderfully in the glorious image and likeness of God who always has you on his mind. He is always thinking good thoughts about you. God wants your future as fulfilled as possible. I alone know the plans I have for you, plans to bring you prosperity and not disaster, plans to bring about the future you hope for – Jeremiah 29:11 (Good News Bible translation)

So, settle in. The Lord knows what He is doing. The gifts and callings are without repentance. That simply means that the gifts which God has bestowed upon us and the calling with which He has favored us will never be revoked. God is a not a man that He should lie neither the son of man that He should repent. If He said it; it shall come to pass.

God does speak to man by His spirit. Whether it is by vision, dream, inward witness, audible voice or by a life experience, you will know the true meaning in the message. The clearest way God speaks is through His word. His word is precise and detailed. It is alive and is spirit and by no means is it confusing! So, be encouraged and be of good cheer. God has not forsaken, nor has He forgotten. He has overcome the world. Get up. Go I say!

Chapter Twenty-three
Far Beyond the Clouds

———∿∿∿———

There is a familiar Hymn by Thomas T. Lynch *Lift Up Your Heads, Rejoice Redemption Draweth Nigh.* Its words are so beautiful: He comes, the wide world's King, He comes, the true heart's Friend, New gladness to begin, and ancient wrong to end; He comes, to fill with light the weary waiting eye; Lift up your heads, rejoice, redemption draweth nigh.

What a happy time to be in our redemptive state; in our glorified bodies. I like every believer look forward to that day of Christ's return. I have assignments to accomplish. You have assignments to finish. We all have our assignments to fulfill, goals to reach, and our duties to perform. As earlier stated, getting the gift of salvation is not just for getting to Heaven. Heaven is not just for milk and honey diets, walking on gold streets, living in Heaven-sized mansions or wearing crowns and diadems. The aim of our existence is to fulfill God's purpose in the earth. Don't just gaze up in the clouds waiting for the Lord to return. Instead, go beyond your thinking into mission and purpose. Don't miss the "clear day" message. "Work while it is day for when the night comes, no man can work (John 9:4)! Go beyond the clouds in your thinking, dreaming, visions and experiences. Get busy. Occupy! Practice! Make your mark in the world. Leave a deposit in the earth through your path to destiny.

Is this your question, "What is destiny and how can I know it for my life?" There is a destiny; a specific plan for you. The answer to the destiny question, it is what you are meant to do, what you are meant to have, and where you are meant to be. How, you ask? You are probably doing destiny (purpose or intention) already. Because if there is a longing in you to do a particular thing, and you can't live without doing it that is probably your thing of purpose, intention or destiny. This is the one thing that brings a *"yeah"* to your soul. If you've always done it and it never becomes stale to you, that's your thing! If you are in your zone when you act, write, paint, teach, preach, sing, play a sport, dance or anything that brings gratitude like nothing else can, then you are probably doing what you were designed to do. You may ask, Louise, I do NOT know what I'm supposed to do in life or even what I am good at. I don't have a talent like you. I don't go to church and pray and all that. I am not a churchy person, I may or may not be a spiritual person, so none of those "read your bible and pray" words connect with me. I don't know how to do that. But I still want to have a productive life.

I will tell you in a nutshell, you still can know your destiny. Pay attention to yourself. What is it that you really like to do? I love to sing and play the piano and write, but I also like PAPER! I love to organize it and file it. Man, for me to work where there is paper, I am in my work zone. You don't have to have protracted prayer and speak in tongues for an hour a day to know what to do in a day or for the rest of your days. All you have to do is PAY ATTENTION. See, God our Creator is so infinite in wisdom that He already put your destiny inside of your spirit. You already know that you are a spirit being living in an earth suit (your body), with a soul. So everything you would ever need for your spirit, soul, and body, you already have.

Watch a child's play. During some course of that play time, you will see the child act out something he's seen before, but he does it so well that people generally say, "Oh he's been here before," or something along those lines. If you have a passion towards children, then you may have the ministry of teaching or child care or something more specific. I guarantee if you search inside diligently for your path, you can discover it. God is a spirit, so for a better understanding, you will have to ask for His assistance through prayer.

My friend, you can know it. You can accomplish it. Work every day by practicing. Like child's play, practice. You'll only increase in knowledge, understanding, and wisdom because God gives the increase. There is some mind-transforming you will HAVE to exercise. God will change your spirit immediately, but changing your mind is a lifetime occupation. If you can get in your spirit the things the Lord thinks about you, this will change your thinking. Your mind will have no choice but to line up with your spirit.

Learn that your end will be great. Even though you will go through pitfalls, trials, and tribulations, you must remain focused on these facts: CHRIST HAS WON US THE VICTORY, THEREFORE WE HAVE, I HAVE, YOU HAVE WON, YOU WILL WIN, YOU ARE A WINNER, and YOU CAN'T LOSE! Remember, you are the head and not the tail; above only and never beneath. You are the seed of Abraham and a joint heir of Jesus, the son of David.

No matter what the enemy brings your way, you won't faint, you won't give up, and you won't lose, because you have put the power of life in your mouth. Death and LIFE are in the power of the tongue. You have what you say. Hide these precepts in your heart and confess them for an expected end. This will please the Lord and you'll see His favor. You will find yourself as the NIKE commercial instructs *DOING IT!*

What you think gives directions to follow. At the end of the day, it is what you choose to do that will catapult you into the destiny His designed just for you.

A famous quote from an unknown source is "No man is an island, no man stands alone." How close are you to your divine destiny? Are you about to miss your divine connection? Is it because of someone else, or you? When you really think about it we alone are responsible for our actions, but we are also our brother's keeper. Don't think for one moment your divine connection is only for you, it is for all those who are connected to you. You have the power to change your environment, to change your world! What will be your view? Are you seated on the bus looking back or running towards the bus as it leaves you? Stop gazing up at the clouds! Get to "doing" your life and that in great abundance!

A Covenant with GOD and Yourself

My Mother declared that I used to sing in the crib. I do not remember that, however I do remember imitating any singing I would hear. I remember vividly pressing and banging on flat surfaces like tabletops, benches and such as if I was actually playing the piano. Along with that I would sing and sing and sing. It was like breathing to me.

I also loved imitating my teachers, and nurses. I connected to these kinds of people because they were smart and fascinating. Having people like that in my formative life helped me. Now, I teach music, sing, play piano and write music. I NEVER struggled with what I would be when I grow up, because I always practiced my vocation as a child. I never wanted to be anything else but a singer or something in music.

I have been a personal care assistant to the ailing, I have a son with Downs Syndrome, and trust a SUSTAH; you have to be called to a lifetime ministry of hospitality, love and care in order to nurture such a wonderful breed.

I have always been a Levite and minstrel. I've played in church settings since age seven, and I have never had a time when I didn't play or didn't want to play or teach or sing unless I was just physically unable.

I do believe I was supposed to be a dancer, but the devout nature of my Mother horrified me that dancing was "OF THE DEVIL!" I hated the concept of that, but that was my mother's truth. As I grew up and I learned that dancing is an intricate part of personal expression and it actually comes from God.

I have heard some people say that they are not sure what their talent is. I am not the expert as RICK WARREN, but I agree with him 100%, knowing what we're meant to do simplifies, focuses, increase motivation and prepare us for eternity! Get to know the Creator. This is your ticket. This is your entrance into whom and what you shall become even throughout eternity. The Creator knows His Creation. He knows what the design is and what the design is there for. Tap in, and make a commitment to look, listen and live your dreams.

Make a declaration with yourself to get to know the Creator. He will be glad to introduce you to your purpose.

I, _____ will go beyond any cloud of despair, discouragement, or any other cloud that will hold me back from the God that works in me. I will stop supposing about things that could happen and go for every opportunity. There is good in me and I will put back into the earth as a legacy. I will stop gazing, wondering what if, and connect with God to learn my specific assignment in life. I partner with Jesus to get my life accomplished.

Date _____

Your Personal Journal

Your Personal Journal

Your Personal Journal

Your Personal Journal

Soundtrack and Words Available

BEYOND THE CLOUDS
A STARTING PLACE FOR ME
© March 7, 2013
LYRICS Louise Smith, Carlisle James, Vernel Edwards
Music - Louise Smith

Verse

Take me beyond what I can imagine
Give me the pulse to make it happen all the more
I need the drive, the hunger and the passion
To accomplish what I was created for

Chorus

Beyond the clouds is just a starting place for me
Beyond the sky is what I can have
There is no limit to the image of the Creator
If I can see it, I can do it
If I believe it, I can have it
Beyond the clouds is just a starting place for me x2

Verse

Before I was framed
God gave me greatness and ambition
Then He told me to go and do not be afraid
His love, His will is a must for this position
And I'll do it until I'm in the grave.

Chorus

Beyond the clouds is a starting place for me
Beyond the sky is what I can have
There is no limit to the image of the Creator
If I can see it, I can do it
If I believe it, I will have it
Beyond the clouds is just a starting place for me x2

Vamp

I say I have all that's destined for me

www.ingramcontent.com/pod-product-compliance
Lightning Source LLC
Chambersburg PA
CBHW071131090426
42736CB00012B/2095